ACADEMICS AND BEYOND

Volume 4, The Best of ACLD

ACADEMICS

Co-edited by

and

AND BEYOND

Selected Papers from the 19th International Conference
of the Association for Children and Adults with Learning Disabilities

WILLIAM M. CRUICKSHANK, Ph.D.

School of Public Health
University of Michigan

ELI TASH

St. Francis Children's Activity and Achievement Center
Milwaukee, Wisconsin

SYRACUSE UNIVERSITY PRESS   1983

Library of Congress Cataloging in Publication Data

Association for Children and Adults with Learning
    Disabilities. International Conference (19th :
    1982 : Chicago, Ill.)
    Academics and beyond.

    (The Best of ACLD ;   )
    Includes bibliographies.
    1. Learning disabilities—Congresses.   I. Cruickshank,
William M.   II. Tash, Eli.   III. Title.   IV. Series.
LC4704.A87   1982   371.96'6   82-19525
ISBN 0-8156-2272-4 (pbk.)

CONTENTS

CONTRIBUTORS

SHELDON T. BOXER, Ph.D., St. Thomas Aquinas College, Sparkill, New York

ANN Y. BRECKENRIDGE-CAMPBELL, Early Childhood Education Program, Chicago, Illinois

CHRISTINE M. CASALE, Ph.D., Mountain View School District, Pasadena, California

BERTTRAM CHIANG, Ph.D., University of Wisconsin-Oshkosh, Wisconsin

LINDA MIXON CLARY, Ph.D., Augusta College, Augusta, Georgia

MARY E. DALE, Ed.D., University of Wisconsin-Oshkosh, Wisconsin

MARIJANET DOONAN, Ph.D., St. Thomas Aquinas College, Sparkill, New York

JANICE R. DUNCAN, Ph.D., Ball State University, Muncie, Indiana

MARILYN J. FENDER, Ph.D., University of Wisconsin-Oshkosh, Wisconsin

PAUL J. GERBER, Ph.D., University of New Orleans, New Orleans, Louisiana

HAROLD G. GRIFFIN, Ph.D., University of New Orleans, New Orleans, Louisiana

KARLA HULL, Holy Names College, Oakland, California

JEAN S. KIDDER, Ed.D, Humboldt State University, Arcata, California

LEONARD STEPHEN KRUSZECKI, Early Childhood Education Center, Oakland, California

BRENDA H. MANNING, Ed.D., University of Georgia, Athens, Georgia

SR. KATHLEEN M. McCANN, Early Childhood Education Center, Oakland, California

GAYLE MINDES, Ed.D., Roosevelt University, Chicago, Illinois

JANE Y. MURDOCK, Ph.D., University of New Orleans, New Orleans, Louisiana

NANCY K. NARON, Ph.D., Chicago EARLY Project, Chicago, Illinois

ANN NEELY, University of Georgia, Athens, Georgia

FREDRICKA K. REISMAN, Ph.D., University of Georgia, Athens, Georgia

STEVEN C. RUSSELL, Ph.D., Bowling Green State University, Bowling Green, Ohio

LAURIE D. SABRIO, Ph.D., New Orleans Parish Schools, New Orleans, Louisiana

KAREN GROVES SHEPPO, Augusta College, Augusta, Georgia

CLARE M. SILVA, Ph.D., Old Dominion University, Norfolk, Virginia

HAROLD W. THORPE, Ed.D., University of Wisconsin-Oshkosh, Wisconsin

MARY LORETTA TREPANIER, Ed.D., University of Michigan-Dearborn, Michigan

BETTY H. YARBOROUGH, Ed.D., Old Dominion University, Norfolk, Virginia

PREFACE

PREFACE

IN 1982, EXTREME CHANGES WERE BEGINNING to take place in the field of special education. Public interest in the education of handicapped children, which had peaked in 1975 with the passage of the Education for All Handicapped Children Act (PL 94-142), was beginning to ebb. In 1982, we sensed the beginning of a slow erosion of public concern for special education. This coincided with the move to dissolve the federal Department of Education and the cutback in federal funds for all education, including programs for handicapped children even though they had never been fully funded.

The sense of excitement and deep concern at the 1982 conference reminded me of the tension and tone of excitement at the 1963 Chicago conference at which ACLD was organized. Groups of parents and professionals from twenty states plus Canada were there because they had a common concern and point of view about the learning potential of children with cerebral dysfunctions. They responded to the call for the conference because their children were denied education opportunities. The school establishment during the 1950s and 60s insisted that children with perceptual or neurological impairments or brain damage could not master academic subjects. The parents and professionals who attended the conference believed just the opposite. "All children can learn, if we can learn how to teach them!" they said. Their children had many different specific learning disabilities; however, they could master language and reading and math, provided special educational strategies were developed to help them "learn how to learn." This called for individualized education programs in some cases; but in all cases, it required learning situations responsive to each child's developmental readiness to learn and to that child's distinctive learning style. These parents and professionals believed that a child's disabilities should be held at arm's length, while his or her latent abilities were stimulated.

During the nineteen years since the first ACLD conference in Chicago, complex questions of definition and of criteria have arisen. Schools have been faced with legal questions about special children's "rights to learn."

How should children with varying types and degrees of brain dysfunction be identified and served? Scholars and administrators began to ask, "Exactly what is a specific learning disability? How do we identify children who have learning disabilities? What types of remedial programs are needed? Does the disability last forever? Does it come and go or change throughout the developmental life of a child? How severe must the disability be in order to qualify for special services?"

The controversies proved to be helpful. Out of them came new insights and innovative strategies for helping children "learn how to learn." ACLD followed up the original 1963 conference with annual international conferences in every large city in America, from Boston to Houston and from San Francisco to Milwaukee. Each of these conferences was an open forum for innovative ideas and practices.

The nineteenth annual international conference was held in Chicago, March 3 — 6, 1982. This conference continued the ACLD policy of providing a forum for all persons concerned with learning disabilities. Educators, attorneys, administrators, psychologists, biologists, and neurologists were invited to discuss their latest ideas and research findings at the conference. The participants were left to determine for themselves the practical value of the presentations.

Hundreds of papers and workshops were presented by parents, professionals, and people with learning disabilities.

The developing concerns and open issues ranged from the curtailment of funds for special education to the quest for a new definition of learning disabilities and quantifiable criteria for eligibility of children for services. Presentations ranged from preventive early education starting at birth to continuing vocational and rehabilitative education for adults.

The 15 selected papers included in Volume 4, *The Best of ACLD*, will give the reader an insight into the multiple strands covered by the conference. Collectively, these papers convey a sense of the open issues, controversial theories, and innovative practices that were discussed.

The selected papers included in this volume also represent a variety of points of view as well as subject matter. No papers concerned with legal issues and funding problems were included. Due to space limitations, the editors have selected papers directed toward the educational scene and others pertaining to psychology and neurophysiological dysfunction. Each is important in its own way, and each contributes to the ever-enlarging body of literature and research in the field of learning disabilities.

For the Editorial Committee for Selected Papers
ELI TASH, CO-CHAIRMAN

ACADEMICS AND BEYOND

Volume 4, The Best of ACLD

COMMUNICATION

Editorial note: Two invitational papers are included in this section. Both were submitted too late to be included in the conference program, but both are concerned with the utilization of single-subject research techniques, language functions, and learning disabilities. The extreme variances within any population of children with learning disabilities makes homogeneity a near if not actual impossibility. Single-subject research appropriately utilized provides a research technique which undoubtedly has value in further understanding the complex issues related to learning disabilities.

Oral Language Disorders of the Learning Disabled
A Single-Subject Approach

Steven C. Russell

WHILE PROGRAMMING EFFORTS, particularly with respect to the mandates of PL 94-142 and the practice of providing an Individualized Education Plan (IEP), have reflected a sensitivity to the unique needs of each learning disabled learner, the heterogeneous nature of the learning disabled population has often been overlooked by those who conduct research in this area. The effect of this has been to create a plethora of research reports which are found to be questionable in their applicability to the individual and to the subgroups (Benton 1978; Pirozzolo 1979; Satz and Morris 1980) within the learning disabled population.

A PROBLEM OF RESEARCH DESIGN

There is little question that research is an important aspect of special education. Not only is it needed to further clarify definitions of subgroups of handicapped individuals dealt with by professionals involved in special education, it is also needed to examine diagnostic procedures, intervention and remediation techniques, and the outcomes of instructional programming for handicapped populations, in particular the learning disabled. As Hallahan (1977) points out, there is little opportunity for such research to be definitive. Past research efforts have only confounded this problem by attempting to treat the learning disabled population as a homogeneous group. This assumption of group research, and the subsequent employment of inferential statistics in the analysis of the data, can not be met with such special needs populations as the learning disabled (Kratochwill, Brody, and Piersel 1979).

M.C. Johnson (1977) discusses the fallacy of group studies when investigating special populations, one of the fallacies being treatment of the groups as homogeneous. Guralnick (1978) explains that researchers working with applied problems tend to analyze group behavior with the result providing little, if any, predictability to the individual child. Hence, the apparent need to begin the study of learning disabled learners as heterogeneous can be seen, particularly if such research is to provide benefits of improved definition, improved and applicable intervention and remediation, and evaluation of programming efforts for the selected subgroup population within the larger learning disabled population.

SINGLE-SUBJECT RESEARCH AS AN ANSWER TO THE PROBLEM OF DESIGN

A significant approach to this problem, albeit rather apolitical but one which has received a great amount of attention recently, is that of single-subject research (Kratochwill, Brody, and Piersel 1979). As advocated by Kratochwill *et al.*, single-subject research should be an integral part of the research endeavor in the field of learning disabilities. They continue by stating the apparent benefit of such a research design — individual case studies which can be compiled, leading to the formulation of hypotheses and future research.

Johnson (1977) suggests that although N = 1 as a research design is currently unusual in educational research, it can yield data that do not oversimplify the situation. Through this method and design, the analysis of results, and the comparison of different cases, can be facilitated by the profiles of each case available from such designs. Johnson suggests, for instance, that it might be found that a disability can be corrected in one case, and that this method of correction found to be useful in this single case might well be applied to another case with little, or no change. However, Johnson cautions the researcher, and practitioner alike, by stating that although the disabilities in both cases may be the same (e.g., both being learning disabled), due to the individual differences between the profiles of each (e.g., one individual having significant auditory processing deficits while the other has significant visual processing deficits; one individual exhibiting significant reading disorders while the other demonstrates little or no reading disorder), the method found to be effective in the first case may have to be adjusted for the second case, in order to be effective.

Various designs for conducting single-subject research have been suggested by Hersen and Barlow (1976), Kratochwill (1978), and Guralnick (1978). Among the designs suggested have been the case study, N = 1, intensive, operant, time-series (Kratochwill, Brody, and Piersel 1979), and multiple-baseline (Hersen and Barlow 1976; Guralnick 1978). These methods suggest the same type of research; however, certain procedures in the design or method of analysis change from one type to another. Moreover, with all of these methods it is necessary to specify the subject(s') characteristics, to specify the treatment variables — if a treatment is employed — and to specify the relationship of the relevant subject(s') characteristics to the observations or treatment variables (Guralnick 1978). In addition, replicability becomes the key to establishing generality with the above designs (Kratochwill, Brody, and Piersel 1979).

As Chassan (1961) has stated in support of single-subject research, each case serves as its own control. Statistically significant results cannot be an artifact of a lack of homogeneity between cases. The common fallacy is to assume a significant effect demonstrated in an extensive (group) design exists for every, or for most, or even an appreciable proportion of the members of the population — as is often the case with much of the learning disability research. This assumption is false. The extensive (group) model does not permit identification of the subject(s') characteristics that accompany the tested effect. Therefore, with special populations, in particular the learning disabled, the need for single-subject research, and recognition of the heterogeneous nature of this population, must be supported. Researchers in this field need to feel the importance of this issue.

Nowhere has this concept been more evident, or more strongly advocated, than in the research conducted by Keogh and her colleagues (Keogh, Major, Reid, Gandara, and Omori 1978; Keogh, Major, Omori, Gandara, and Reid 1980; Keogh, Major, Omori, and Reid 1980). Keogh and her associates designed a three-phase, three-year, project to "identify, define operationally, test, and evaluate a set of 'marker variables' which can be used to guide empirical research and program evaluation" (Keogh, Major, Omori, and Reid 1980). Marker variables were defined as generally referring to a common core of characteristics and information regarding samples on which research is being conducted within the confines of a particular field, in this case learning disabilities. More specifically, "Marker variables reflect the constructs which characterize a particular field and may tap cognitive, psychological, social, motoric, or demographic dimensions." The inherent value of marker variables for the learning disability field is nearly implicit in their description. Marker variables "will facilitate the development of a reference base for researchers and program administrators in order that they may compare research findings, generalize results, develop theories, and reach policy decisions."

Though the method chosen by Keogh and her associates for the identification of marker variables was through the use of an extensive review of previous research studies in the field of learning disabilities, followed by refinement of the marker variables, and concluded with a field test of the usefulness of these variables, additional variables of this sort, particularly those not yet identified within the existing body of research, can be discovered and identified through the use of single-subject research. Additionally, both extensive (group) research and single-subject research will profit through the employment of marker variables in that the applicability of the results will be more clearly delineated.

Finally, though it is recognized that the results of such investigations as those that employ a single-subject research design will not be generalizable to the entire population of learning disabled learners, nor to a significant proportion of this population, the results will provide the bases of future research through the generation of hypotheses that will subsequently be testable in experimental designs. Through the generation of these hypotheses, and the subsequent testing on a larger population of like learning disabled learners, it will be possible to define new variables that will assist in the definition, identification, intervention and remediation, and program evaluation of the learning disabled population and education.

A topic of concern where such an approach as that of single-subject research needs consideration is that of the oral language competence of learning disabled children.

LEARNING DISABILITIES: LANGUAGE AND COMMUNICATION DEFICITS

Professionals such as Cruickshank, Bentzen, Ratzeburg, and Tannhauser (1961), and Myklebust (1954) acknowledged early in the history of the field of learning disabilities that children with learning disabilities may exhibit language and communication deficits. Early literature in psychology and linguistics supports this suggestion, although at the time the field of learning disabilities per se was not yet conceived. This is not to suggest that those who would eventually be associated with, and upon whose research would be founded, the field of learning disabilities, were not involved in the study of disorders of spoken language. This is evidenced by the work of Gall in 1802, Bouillaud in 1825, Broca in 1861, Jackson in 1864, Wernicke in 1881, and others. See Wiederholt's (1974) article in *The second review of special education* for an extensive discussion of this literature. For example, M. E. Smith (1933, reprinted in Bloom 1978, pp. 31-38) described a child displaying language problems who might today be classified learning disabled.

> One small boy who was observed at different ages from eighteen months to five-and-a-half years was a particularly crooked talker at four years and ten of these errors occurred in records of his conversation taken at three years ten months and at four years four months. He was backward in talking and his earlier records consisted of only or mainly one-word sentences where word order errors would have small chance of occurring. At the time he started to print, he showed some tendency to mirror-writing and now, at almost twelve years, he reverses the order of letters in his spelling. Examples of word-order errors by this boy are: "Where you did hide?" "This I want." "See 'em dere in," and by others, "Eat soup warm." (From the reprint in Bloom, 1978, pp. 36-37)

In addition, recent research reported by Bloom (1979), and Blank, Gessner, and Esposito (1979) lend support to this notion. Bloom reports a child studied from the age of two years, nine months to approximately five years, displaying language disorders. At the time of this report, the child was eight years old, and in his third year in a classroom for children with learning disabilities. (It should be noted here that this may indeed be the first account of a learning disabled child intensively studied, in terms of his communicative competence, during the primary years of language acquisition. As it is currently difficult to assign the term "learning disabled" to a child before the school years, this type of investigation, studying the learning disabled child as he develops language, can only happen by chance.)

Blank *et al*. (1979) report a case study of a child who displays age appropriate expression of syntactic-semantic relations, but is almost totally ineffective in interpersonal communication. "His difficulties in the use of language for communication were mirrored from infancy by a serious failure either to understand or produce non-verbal communication (e.g., gestures)" (Blank, Gessner, and Esposito 1979, p. 329). Additionally, and perhaps most importantly, there is some indication that the subject of this study might be classified as learning disabled.

> John's history indicated a number of possible signs of difficulty, but there was no firm evidence of any disability. Several professional personnel ... agreed that the available diagnostic categories ... were unsuitable or insufficient to classify his behaviour. Neurological and EEG testing carried out at the time of referral revealed no noticeable abnormalities. Speculations, however, were raised by the neurologist that the behavioural symptoms in aggregate were suggestive of the elusive syndrome of *"minimal cerebral dysfunction."* [emphasis added] (p. 331)

Hence, the professional finds support for the notion that the learning disabled child may often exhibit language and communication deficits.

PREVIOUS INVESTIGATIONS REGARDING THE LANGUAGE AND COMMUNICATION DEFICITS OF THE LEARNING DISABLED

Subsequent to the acknowledgment that learning disabled children may display language and communication deficits, it was acknowledged that language plays a significant role in academic achievement (Cruickshank *et al.* 1961; Myklebust 1954). This realization inspired studies concerning language deficits and the learning disabled population (Rosenthal 1970; Wiig and Semel 1973; Wiig, Semel, and Crouse 1973; Vogel 1974; Wiig and Semel 1974; Parker, Freston, and Drew 1975; Semel and Wiig 1975; Wiig and Roach 1975; Wiig and Semel 1975; Wiig, Lapointe, and Semel 1977).

The methods for assessing the language deficits of the learning disabled children in these studies were many and include: Menyuk's testing approach using prescribed questions, imitations, and sentence completions (Rosenthal 1970); Berko's experimental test of morphology (Wiig, Semel, and Crouse 1973); the *Illinois Test of Psycholinguistic Abilities* (Wiig, Semel, and Crouse 1973; Vogel 1974; Wiig and Semel 1974; Wiig, Lapointe, and Semel 1977); the *Wiig-Semel Test of Linguistic Concepts* (Wiig and Semel 1973; Wiig, Lapointe, and Semel 1977); Lee's *Northwest Syntax Screening Test* (Vogel 1974; Semel and Wiig 1975; Wiig, Lapointe, and Semel 1977); measures devised by Berry, Lee and Canter, and Vogel (Vogel 1974); the *Wechsler Intelligence Scale for Children* (Wiig and Semel 1974); the *Stanford Achievement Test* (Wiig and Semel 1974); logico-grammatical sentences (Wiig and Semel 1974); the *Assessment of Children's Language Comprehension* (Semel and Wiig 1975); twelve lists of five stimulus words by Freston and Drew (Parker, Freston, and Drew 1975); *Newcombe-Marshall Sentences* (Wiig and Roach 1975; Wiig, Lapointe, and Semel 1977); the Verbal Opposites subtest from the *Detroit Tests of Learning Aptitude* (Wiig and Semel 1975; Wiig, Lapointe, and Semel 1977); Visual Configuration Naming (Wiig and Semel 1975; Wiig, Lapointe, and Semel 1977), the Rating Scale Profile (Wiig and Semel 1975), and an adaptation of the Fluency of Controlled Association subtest (Wiig and Semel 1975; Wiig, Lapointe, and Semel 1977) all from the *Boston Diagnostic Aphasia Examination*; Producing Sentences and Defining Words subtests from the *Minnesota Test for Differential Diagnosis of Aphasia* (Wiig and Semel 1975; Wiig, Lapointe, and Semel 1977); and the *Token Test* (Wiig, Lapointe, and Semel 1977).

These studies have suggested that the learning disabled child with language deficits "may be assigned to one or more of four broad categories. They may reflect either (1) reductions in short-term memory, (2) delays in the acquisition of linguistic rules and in linguistic processing of spoken language, (3) reductions in the cognitive-semantic and logical processing of spoken language, and/or (4) dysnomia, characterized by reduced accuracy and speed of retrieval of words and verbal associations" (Wiig 1976, p.5).

The above studies — in particular those of Wiig and Roach (1975), Wiig and Semel (1974, 1975), and Wiig, Lapointe, and Semel (1977) — also indicate that the language deficits of learning disabled children may indeed continue into adolescence.

However important these findings may be, the above studies mirror the studies of normal child language acquisition and the studies of the language disordered child that were "consistent with the generative grammatical emphasis of the 1960s ... primarily syntactic analyses of sentences ... produced spontaneously or imitatively . . . focused on the child's linguistic competence or knowledge of language structure, and not his communicative competence, his appropriate and effective use of those structures in specific contexts'' (Gallagher and Darnton 1978, pp. 118-119). As pointed out by Bloom and Lahey (1978), most aspects of use (pragmatics) are not assessed through the employment of standardized assessment instruments. Although standardized assessment instruments may be used to describe content (semantics) and form (syntactics), direct observation of the subject in a spontaneous speech sample is necessary for the assessment of use (pragmatics). It is through this type of assessment, direct observation, that it is possible to see the child using language for communicative interaction, and to see the child using language for natural purposes, rather than for elicitation or imitation. This type of analysis of the oral language output of the learning disabled child was called for in the writings of Mercer in 1979.

Beyond this criticism of the previous research on the language deficits of learning disabled children, due to the methodology employed, an additional criticism may be made against the abovementioned studies. In these studies, the subjects have often been defined no further than to state that they are classified as learning disabled (with counterparts labeled as normal). If indeed there is further classification made, it is at best minimal. With the concerns raised above regarding the need for clear, concise definition of the subjects under study and appropriate use of research designs, it can be easily seen that the value of the abovementioned studies has added little to our understanding of specific children within the learning disabled population. While these studies may provide information regarding the learning disabled population as a whole, they provide us with little information concerning the oral language deficits of the various subgroups of the learning disabled, nor do they provide us with usable information regarding clarification of definition, clarification of diagnostic procedures, application of intervention and remediation strategies, or evaluation of programming efforts.

RECENT INVESTIGATIONS REGARDING THE LANGUAGE AND COMMUNICATION DEFICITS OF THE LEARNING DISABLED

Several recent investigations (e.g., Donahue, Pearl, and Bryan 1980; Bryan, Donahue, and Pearl 1981a; Bryan, Donahue, and Pearl 1981b; Donahue 1981) have been conducted which examine the characteristics of the learning disabled with regard to their communicative competence, in particular their ability to use (pragmatics) language effectively in an interactional setting. For example, Donahue, Pearl, and Bryan (1980), using a referential communication task, examined learning disabled children's ability to initiate repair of a breakdown in communication using conversational rules. Messages, varying in the adequacy of the information which they contained, were employed. The subjects, both learning disabled and normal, were placed in the role of listener and required to select referents based on the messages. Subjects classified as learning disabled were found to be less likely to request clarification of messages that were inadequate in their informational content. Likewise, the learning disabled children were found to make fewer referent choices that were correct than did their normal counterparts. Finally, this investigation suggested that the failure of the learning disabled subjects to initiate repair of a communicative breakdown, or to request clarification of inadequate messages, was not due to linguistic deficits alone. Instead, it was suggested that this inability to deal effectively with inadequate messages was related to pragmatic deficits, more specifically, the learning disabled subjects' understanding of the conversational rules for repairing such communicative breakdowns.

In another investigation (Donahue 1981), the pragmatic competence of learning disabled children was again examined. This investigation was designed in a manner which would allow assessment of both linguistic and social knowledge. This was accomplished by designing the study to examine the ability of learning disabled children to employ appropriate politeness and persuasive strategies with regard to the status of the listener to whom such strategies were addressed. Using a task which involved making requests of four imaginary listeners who varied in their intimacy and power relationships to both the learning disabled and normal subjects, it was found that in comparison to normal girls, learning disabled girls made more polite requests. Regarding the learning disabled boys, it was found that they were limited both in the variety of their persuasive appeals and in the degree to which those appeals indicated higher levels of listener perspective taking. Furthermore, it was found that learning disabled boys varied their politeness and persuasive appeals as a function of listener features; however, this was accomplished by addressing different dimensions than those addressed by the normal boys' requests. Finally, it was suggested that even though the learning disabled boys did not appear deficient in the linguistic forms used for indicating politeness, they did produce fewer appropriate request strategies than their counterparts, the normal boys.

While each of these studies (Donahue et al. 1980; Bryan et al. 1981a; Bryan et al. 1981b; Donahue 1981) have indeed begun to explore the communicative competence of the learning disabled, and thereby, respond to the criticism of previous research which has focused on the child's linguistic knowledge, each suffers from the more basic criticism — treatment of the learning disabled population as homogeneous, and a lack of specification of the population under study. As each of these investigations utilized the same subject selection criteria, it is necessary to examine but one to see what is meant here.

In the investigation conducted by Donahue, Pearl, and Bryan (1980), subjects were selected from grades 1 through 8 in a Chicago parochial school system — a school system that does *not* identify those who are learning disabled. Further, participation by "learning disabled" subjects was based on intelligence test scores — a score of at least 90 on the *Peabody Picture Vocabulary Test* (PPVT) (Dunn 1965), teacher ratings (i.e., those "having difficulty in reading, paying attention, acquiring verbal skills, or following directions" (Donahue *et al.* 1980, p. 391)), and reading achievement test scores (below the 40th percentile for grade level as measured by the *SRA Achievement Series Test* (Naslund, Thorpe, and Lefever 1978)), or for those whom this measure was not available, the reading subtest of the *Woodcock-Johnson Psycho-Educational Battery* (Woodcock and Johnson 1977) was used. Normal subjects were defined as those who "received average or above average teacher ratings and reading achievement scores above the 40th percentile" (Donahue *et al.* 1980, p. 391), and as randomly selected classmates matching the learning disabled on school attended, grade placement, and sex. All subjects were Caucasian, predominantly middle-class, and native speakers of English.

When pondering such selection criteria numerous questions come to mind. Do all of the subjects of such study have the same deficit/disorder? Do all subjects exhibit their deficit/disorder to the same degree? What variance would be seen if one were to examine more complete profiles regarding each subject, for instance historical background — educational, developmental, and medical; results of processing tests — e.g., the *Illinois Test of Psycholinguistic Abilities* (Kirk, McCarthy, and Kirk 1968), the *Motor-Free Test of Visual Perception* (Colarusso and Hammill 1972); complete *Woodcock-Johnson Psycho-Educational Battery* (Woodcock and Johnson 1977) profiles; more complete measures of intelligence — e.g., the *Wechsler Intelligence Scale for Children-Revised* (Wechsler 1974); more complete assessment of academic achievement; and, possible consideration of environmental variables — e.g., home life? How different are these "learning disabled" subjects from those children who receive remedial reading instruction but are not found to be learning disabled? Would these "learning disabled" subjects represent one subgroup of the larger population or a variety of subgroups?

The answers to these inquiries can not be found through such subject selection and identification procedures. The result of such subject selection procedures is the continuation of the notion that the learning disabled population is one which is homogeneous — all those who suffer from reading disabilities. In the end, the results of such investigations lend little to our definition, intervention and remediation efforts, and understanding because they can not, as the authors attempt to do, be generalized to a heterogeneous population.

In effect, though it may be commendable that these investigations have at least limited their study to those with reading disorders, one is still faced with many questions, as voiced above, regarding the exact nature of the population under study and the degree of variance within this population. Again, we are faced with the fallacies iterated by Johnson (1977), Kratochwill *et al.* (1979), Chassan (1961), Guralnick (1978), and Keogh *et al.* (1978, 1980, 1980).

LANGUAGE AND COMMUNICATION DEFICITS AS SEEN THROUGH A SINGLE-SUBJECT RESEARCH DESIGN

In contrast to the abovementioned studies of the learning disabled and their language and communication deficits, Russell (1981) designed a study to explore descriptively the differences in the oral language production of learning disabled children in comparison to normal children that (1) would employ well-defined subjects, and, (2) would be undertaken via observable spontaneous interaction.

Subgroups of the Learning Disabled

The relationship between auditory and visual perceptual dysfunctions and learning disabilities has long been recognized (Cruickshank 1966, 1977; Johnson and Myklebust 1967; Tarnopol 1969; Bush and Waugh 1976; Mann, Goodman, and Wiederholt 1978). Hallahan (1975, p. 31), in summarizing several studies concerning visual perceptual problems (Leton 1962; Davol and Hastings 1967; Coleman 1968; Lyle 1968; Whipple and Kodman 1969; Skubic and Anderson 1970), states that the "evidence strongly suggests that learning-disabled children, as a group, perform poorly on tasks designed to assess visual perceptual abilities." Hallahan and Kauffman (1978, p. 138), in citing investigations regarding the auditory perceptual abilities of learning disabled children (Golden and Steiner 1969; Lingren 1969; Flynn and Byrne 1970), state that these investigations "indicate that auditory perceptual difficulties are more often found in learning-disabled than in normal children."

However strongly the evidence might suggest that learning disabled children have visual and/or auditory perceptual dysfunctions, caution must be used in ascribing these characteristics to the entire population of learning disabled children. Hallahan and Kauffman (1978, p. 139) state that "caution must be maintained in considering the significance of these results. These studies . . . are based on *groups* of children. In other words, not all children with reading problems [or learning disabilties] have perceptual deficits, and some children who have perceptual deficits can read adequately."

Support for these two subgroups within the learning disabled population is also found in the definitional statement authored by Wepman, Cruickshank, Deutsch, Morency, and Strother (1975) — a definition which is more extensively descriptive than that contained in PL 94-142. This definition focuses on perceptual or perceptual-motor handicaps which cause a deficit in academic achievement. The definition does not specify an etiology or contributing factors, but does suggest a neurological dysfunction relating to perceptual processes. In addition, it allows for the specification of subgroups (e.g., those with auditory processing deficits, and those with visual processing deficits) within the larger population of learning disabled, i.e., "impairment of perception may distort or disturb the cellular system and/or the normal function of one or more sensory systems," (Wepman et al. 1975, p. 306).

Visual and Auditory Processing Deficits, and Language

The question then arises as to whether or not one could reasonably expect to find that a visual perceptual dysfunction would influence language and communication abilities differently than an auditory perceptual dysfunction.

First, a consideration of the relationship between visual perception and language will be presented: "The ability to relate perception and language is one of the most important functions of our cognitive system ... there are similarities between our linguistic and perceptual representations that may have arisen from a basic conceptual organization of space" (Clark, Carpenter, and Just 1973, p. 376). Frostig and Maslow (1969) wrote, "Cross-sectional studies show that at least 15 to 25 percent of children in the beginning school grades suffer from perceptual disabilities, language difficulties and sensory-motor dysfunctions, or a combination of these disabilities" (p. 222). Wiig and Austin (1972) presented data to exhibit that several of their subjects, children with central language disorders, showed significant visual attentional deficits. Allen (1974), examining the relationship between visual perception and oral language production of young children, found that visual perception processes contributed significantly to the explanation of the variance among his subjects of some skills in all four aspects (connected discourse, syntactic skills, morphological skills, and associative skills) of oral language sampled. Allen found that "Spatial Relationships," on the Marianne Frostig *Developmental Test of Visual Perception* (DTVP), was the most consistent contributor to morphological and associative skills, and "Constancy of Shape" (DTVP) most often contributed significantly to syntactic skills. These findings suggest, in the very least, a partial relationship between visual perception and oral language. See Russell (1981) for an extensive review of this literature.

Turning to the relationship between auditory perception and language, Myklebust (1954, pp. 9-15) states: "Young children with disturbed auditory behavior present problems primarily because of their inadequate language development . . . . Language incapacity is the common basis for all of the auditory disorders in infants and young children . . . to acquire language the child must have adequate hearing and intactness of the central nervous system. The child who is peripherally deaf and the child with brain damage that interferes with the interpretation of sound will both fail to acquire speech, but for different reasons."

Tallal (1976), in citing the conclusion of a previous experiment (Tallal and Piercy, 1975) comments that a primary impairment in auditory temporal processing may be the basis of some language disorders. Again, the literature suggests a relationship between auditory perception and oral language. See Russell (1981) for an extensive review of this literature.

With the above concerns and research as a background, the specific intent of the present study was to define the following question: If two learning disabled children — one evidencing visual processing/perceptual deficits, the other auditory processing/perceptual deficits — and one normal child were compared with respect to their oral language output — syntactic, semantic, and pragmatic — in spontaneous conversational interaction, would there be a significant difference between the oral language output of the three subjects?

METHOD

Subjects

The three subjects of this investigation were selected from the school age population of a public, metropolitan school district within the Midwest. All three subjects were Caucasian, and native speakers of Standard American English (SAE), male, and ranged in age from 8-8 to 9-3. All three subjects were examined by an opthalmologist and were found to be within normal limits and with no abnormalities on the Goldmann Field Test. The three subjects were also examined by an audiologist; this testing revealed normal results for both Mark V. and John N. The third subject, Matthew A., was found to have a bilateral, high frequency, sensorineural loss; however, it was determined that this loss would not likely interfere with the acquisition of language. In addition, the three subjects represented the same basic socioeconomic status, middle-class.

Two of the subjects of this study were identified as *learning disabled*, Matthew A. who exhibited auditory processing deficits, and Mark V. who exhibited visual processing deficits. John N., the third subject, was the *normal control*.

All subjects had FSIQ scores on the WISC-R within the average range (89 to 110). In addition, the learning disabled subjects, Matthew A. and Mark V., had a discrepancy equal to or greater than ten points between their PIQ and their VIQ.

Other psychoeducational measures employed in the selection and identification of the subjects included the *Illinois Test of Psycholinguistic Abilities-Revised*, the *Motor-Free Test of Visual Perception*, the *Auditory Discrimination Test*, the *Developmental Test of Visual-Motor Integration*, the *Wide Range Achievement Test*, the *Jordan Left-Right Reversal Test-Revised*, and selected portions of the *Woodcock-Johnson Psycho-Educational Battery*. As was expected, subjects performed on the psychoeducational measures in accordance with their disability or lack of it; Matthew A. scored below the norm on those measures of auditory processing, Mark V. scored below the norm on those measures of visual processing, and John N. scored at or above the norm. Two exceptions were noted. John N. did score below the norm for three Auditory Vocal subtests, and one Visual Motor subtest of the ITPA. Finally, Matthew A. did not score at or above the norm on the *Developmental Test of Visual-Motor Integration*.

In addition, a large volume of data was collected on each of the subjects from their school records, medical records, and from family interviews. Significant findings pertaining to each subject will be summarized here.

Matthew A. Matthew's Mother reported that he did not say words until the age of three. Medical reports concerning Matthew indicated a history of bilateral severe serous otitis media, requiring myringotomies and ventilating tubes on two occasions. It was also reported in both school records and in the medical records that Matthew's academic achievement suffered from severe auditory association deficits, auditory discrimination and memory deficits, and an inability to transfer from acoustic symbol systems to graphic symbol systems.

Mark V. Mark's Mother indicated that Mark seemed to have no concept or sense of time. Other than a reported syncopal attack, medical records did not report anything unusual. School records indicated that Mark had difficulty recognizing certain letters, and sight words; further, it was indicated that he reversed letters and numbers, and displayed difficulty with visual motor perception. Finally, it was indicated that Mark had poor organizational skills, strengths in auditory areas, and weaknesses in visual areas of performance.

John N. Data accumulated concerning John from his Mother, medical records, and school records did not reveal anything unusual. It might be best said that he characterized the normal, average child.

Procedure

The procedure consisted of the collection of spontaneous language samples in dyadic interactions. Each subject was audiotaped and videotaped in conversational interaction during three different sessions, with three partners — experimenter, peer, and mother — one in each session. Each sesssion was one hour in length, and took place in a studio containing a set of common age-appropriate toys, books, furniture, and games. The only constraint placed on the interaction was that subjects and their partners were instructed to begin each session with a puppet play, maintained for approximately 15 minutes. This constraint was employed to motivate and initiate interaction between the subject and the participant.

ANALYSES

Transcription

A total of three hours of spontaneous conversational interaction for each subject constituted the initial data base — one hour in conversation for each subject with each of the conversational partners, experimenter, peer, and mother. This primary data base was reduced to a total of one-and-one-half hours for each subject, reducing the sample with each partner to 30 minutes, by deleting the first and final 15 minutes of each one-hour sample. The rationale for this was that the center-most 30 minutes would be more likely to be representative of the communicative competence of the subjects, and be more interactive, not suffering from the difficulties of initiating a conversation or from fatigue of the participants.

Orthographic transcription of the verbal portion of the communicative interaction was obtained from the audiotapes; nonverbal portions were then added, and were obtained from the videotapes. Completed transcriptions for each subject by experimenter, peer, and mother interactions included all utterances, notation of other vocalizations, notation of totally and partially unintelligible utterances, nonverbal behaviors associated with utterances, and information concerning the context in which the interactions occurred.

Linguistic Maturity

Several measures of linguistic maturity were calculated for each subject. The measures included Brown's Mean Length of Utterance (Brown 1973);

McCarthy's Mean Length of Response (Johnson, Darley, and Spriestersbach 1963); Davis' Mean of Five Longest Responses (Johnson *et al.* 1963);
and the Number of One-Word Responses (Johnson *et al.* 1963).

Syntactic Analysis

As a measure of the language structure or grammatical complexity exhib-
itied by the subjects, the McCarthy-Davis system for classifying utterances was
employed (Johnson *et al.* 1963). This system is composed of two major categories — utterances considered to be Complete Responses and those considered to
be Incomplete Responses. Complete Responses include Functionally Complete But Structurally Incomplete; Simple Sentences Without Phrases; Simple
Sentences With Phrases, or With Compound Subject, Predicate, or Object;
Complex and Compound Sentences; and, Elaborated Sentences. Incomplete
Responses is not subdivided; however, this category includes responses that are
incomprehensible or fragmentary, those where a constituent (e.g., a verb) is
omitted, those that are interrupted and entail a subsequent form change, and
those that are left uncompleted.

Semantic Analysis

In order to examine the semantic concepts encoded by the subjects in
their utterances, Bloom and Lahey's Twenty-One Semantic Categories (Bloom
and Lahey 1978) were employed. These categories include Existence, Non-
existence, Recurrence, Rejection, Denial, Attribution, Possession, Action,
Locative Action, Locative State, State, Quantity, Notice, Time, Coordinate,
Causality, Dative, Specifier, Epistemic, Mood, and Antithesis.

Semantic/Syntactic, or Content/Form Analysis

In order to characterize the interaction between these two areas of linguistic productivity, semantics and syntax, Bloom and Lahey's grid for
Content/Form (Bloom and Lahey 1978) was employed. This grid employs
the same Twenty-One Semantic Categories listed above. In addition, each
category is defined by a developmental scheme consisting of eight phases.
Each phase within a category is further defined by the necessary constituents
to be placed in that phase, e.g., Dative, Phase Five, noun plus noun; Dative,
Phase Six, noun plus noun plus preposition "to" or "for." Criteria for productive use of a phase/category was set at eight to ten occurrences within
the sample of a subject.

Pragmatic Analysis

Gallagher's Model (Gallagher 1978) of Conversational Analysis was employed here to examine the pragmatic features of oral language production exhibited by the subjects of this study. The purpose of such an analysis is to characterize the communicative competence of the subjects by inspecting their adherence to the rules of conversation evidenced in spontaneous communicative interaction.

This model consists of two categories — Utterance Pairs, and Topical Units. The category Utterance Pairs includes Comment and Acknowledgement (further subdivided into Stereotyped Acknowledgement, Repetition Acknowledgement, Extension Acknowledgement, and Extension-Repetition Acknowledgement); Comment and Contingent Query (further subdivided into Request for Confirmation, Neutral Contingent Query, and Request for Specific Constituent Repetition); Contingent Query and Response (further subdivided into Yes-No, Repetition, Elaboration Revision, Reduction Revision, Phonetic Change Revision, and Substitution Revision); and, Request and Answer (further analyzed for structure, sincerity, and directness of the request).

Only those topics which were successfully established were analyzed via Topical Units. Those topics that were successfully established were examined for (1) the way in which they were established (e.g., overt markers, statements, questions); (2) the number of speaker-turns necessary for establishment of a topic; (3) the number of topics successfully established by both the subjects and the participants; (4) the number of turns at speaking within topics by both subjects and participants; and, (5) the way in which subjects related to an established topic (either collaborative or incorporative).

Reliability

Both transcriptions and the utterance scoring were evaluated. Comparisons for the purposes of reliability were based on approximately 10 percent of the data base. These segments were re-transcribed and re-scored by an independent observer.

Re-transcription and re-scoring by the independent observer yielded a high percentage of agreement with the original transcription and scoring by the experimenter, ranging from approximately 97.4 percent for the transcription of Nonverbal Behavior to 73.3 percent for the scoring of Topical Units.

RESULTS

Because the results of this investigation are too numerous and detailed to be discussed within the confines of this paper, the reader is referred to Russell (1981) for a complete discussion. Only highlights of the results will be presented here.

A total of 820 language events were obtained for Matthew A., 1,014 for Mark V., and 1,199 for John N. These served as the data to be analyzed.

Linguistic Maturity

Results of the analyses for linguistic maturity indicated that Matthew A. scored lowest on these measures, followed by Mark V., and finally, John N. (e.g., the over-all mean of McCarthy's Mean of the Longest Response for Matthew A. was 4.17, for Mark V. 4.87, and for John N. 5.19).

Syntactic Complexity

Results of the analysis for syntactic complexity (McCarthy-Davis system for classifying utterances) indicated that Matthew A. uttered simple syntactic constructions with a percentage frequency of 41 percent, and complex syntactic constructions with a percentage frequency of 13 percent; that Mark V. uttered simple syntactic constructions with a percentage frequency of 48 percent, and complex syntactic constructions with a percentage frequency of 15 percent; and, that John N. uttered simple syntactic constructions with a percentage frequency of 40 percent, and complex syntactic constructions with a percentage frequency of 20 percent.

Semantic Encoding

The analysis for semantic encoding using Bloom and Lahey's Twenty-One Semantic Categories did not yield any noteworthy results.

Semantic/Syntactic Analysis

Results of the analysis of the interaction between semantics and syntax (using Bloom and Lahey's grid) indicated that Matthew A. exhibited productive use at the highest category/phase in 16 of the 21 categories; that Mark V. exhibited productive use in 13 of the 21 categories at the highest category/phase; and, that John N. exhibited productive use at the highest category/phase in 19 of the 21 categories.

Pragmatic Analysis

Utterance pair — comment and acknowledgment

It was found that Matthew A. most often used Stereotyped Acknowledgements (20 percent) when verbally acknowledging the comments of his partners, and that 52 percent of the comments of his partners were not verbally acknowledged by him. On the other hand, it was found that Mark V. most often used Extension Acknowledgements (26 percent), and that 47 percent of the comments of his partners were not verbally acknowledged by him. Finally, it was found that John N. most often used Extension Acknowledgements (43 percent), but only 9 percent of the comments of his partners were not verbally acknowledged by him.

Utterance pair — contingent query and response

Although Matthew A. used all of the types of response with the exception of Phonetic Change Revision, he most often used a Yes-No response (40 percent) when responding to contingent queries made by his partners; in addition, 22 percent of the contingent queries made by his conversational partners did not receive a verbal response. Again, Mark V. also most often used the Yes-No response (56 percent), and was noted to have not responded to 24 percent of the contingent queries made by his conversational partners. Finally, John N. also was found to have used the Yes-No response most often (57 percent); however, he did respond to all contingent queries made by his partners.

Topical units

Results of the analysis of the Topical Units indicated that Matthew A. initiated fewer topics (32 percent) than did his partners (68 percent), that when he did initiate the topic it contained fewer turns ($\overline{X}$ 8.17) than when initiated by his partners ($\overline{X}$ 12.35), and was most often established by the use of overt markers (34 percent). Results indicated that the mean number of turns for the establishment of a topic was greater for Matthew (1.46) than for his partners (1.13). Additionally, results indicated that Matthew's turns were more often Collaborative (89 percent when the topic was subject-initiated, 93 percent when partner-initiated) than Incorporative (11 percent when the topic was subject initiated, 7 percent when partner-initiated), and that he was less likely to collaborate or incorporate when the topic was subject-initiated (21 percent) than when the topic was partner-initiated (79 percent).

Results of the analysis of Topical Units indicated that Mark V. initiated fewer topics (39 percent) than did his partners (61 percent), that when he did initiate the topic it contained fewer turns ($\overline{X}$ 6.06) than when initiated by his partners ($\overline{X}$ 8.53), and was most often established by the use of questions (45 percent). Results further indicated that the mean number of turns for the establishment of a topic was greater for Mark (1.38) than for his partners (1.04). In addition, results indicated that Mark's turns were more often Collaborative (87 percent when the topic was subject-initiated, 86 percent when partner-initiated) than Incorporative (13 percent when the topic was subject-initiated, 14 percent when partner-initiated), and that Mark V. waa less likely to collaborate or incorporate when the topic was subject-initiated (27 percent) than when the topic was partner-initiated (73 percent).

Finally, results of the analysis of the Topical Units indicated that John N. initiated nearly the same number of topics (50 percent) as did his partners (50 percent), that when he initiated the topic it contained a greater number of turns ($\overline{X}$ 10.66) than when initiated by his partners ($\overline{X}$ 8.79), and was most often established by the use of statements (64 percent). Furthermore, results indicated that the mean number of turns for the establishment of a topic was less for John (1.03) than for his partners (1.15). Results indicated that John's turns were more often Collaborative (80 percent when the topic was subject-initiated, 84 percent when partner-initiated) than Incorporative (20 percent when subject-initiated, 16 percent when partner-initiated), and that John was as likely to collaborate or incorporate when the topic was subject-initiated (51 percent) as when the topic was partner-initiated (49 percent).

DISCUSSION

Though only skeletal results could be presented here, in the very least it should be clear that auditory processing deficits and visual processing deficits do affect the language and communication abilities of the subjects in this study. In comparison, since variables other than academic achievement and the processing deficits exhibited by the learning disabled subjects were controlled for, this does not seem too strong a conclusion to draw. Certainly, it is in line with the suggestions of Clark, Carpenter, and Just (1973), Frostig and Maslow (1969), Wiig and Austin (1972), Allen (1974), Myklebust (1954), Tallal (1976), and Tallal and Piercy (1975). It is apparent from the results presented, the learning disabled subjects were functioning at lower levels in all areas of concern in conversational interaction than was the normal subject.

However, upon closer examination of the data, additional suggestions may be drawn. It is interesting to note that Matthew A. would appear at the lowest end of a continuum, followed by Mark V., and then John N., at the highest end, for linguistic maturity. Again, the same exact continuum could be constructed when considering syntactic development. Were the subjects placed on a continuum for semantic/syntactic encoding, Mark V. would appear at the lowest end, followed by Matthew A., and finally, John N. at the highest end. Finally, were the three subjects placed on a continuum for pragmatic competence, both Matthew A. and Mark V. would appear together at the lowest end, and John N. would appear at the high end. Though the ordering is suggested by the present data, the evidence contained herein does not make it possible to construct such continua; this will have to await further investigations. Still, it is notable that the learning disabled child with auditory processing deficits (Matthew A.) seems to be affected in the areas of linguistic maturity and syntactic development, and that, on the other hand, the learning disabled child with visual processing deficits (Mark V.) seems to be affected in the area of semantic/syntactic encoding. Both learning disabled children seem to be affected in the area of pragmatic competence.

This suggestion leads to the hypothesis that processing disorders, visual and auditory, differentially affect language and communication abilities. Though this can not be generalized to the entire population of learning disabled children, nor to even these two subgroups of learning disabled children, it does seem to apply to the subjects of this study. And, it casts doubt on the findings of previous research on the language and communication deficits of the learning disabled which have tended to treat this population as one which is homogeneous. Future research will need to be conducted to further examine the affects of processing deficits on the language and communication abilities of the learning disabled population.

If such findings as these are corroborated by future research, implications will be forthcoming for the training of teachers to serve the learning disabled population, for remedial and compensatory programming efforts, and for definitional statements.

REFERENCES

Allen, J. C. Relationships between visual perception and oral language production of young children. *Perceptual and Motor Skills*, 1974, *38*, 1319-1327.

Benton, A. Some conclusions about dyslexia. In A. Benton & D. Pearl (Eds.), *Dyslexia: An appraisal of current knowledge*. New York: Oxford University Press, 1978.

Blank, M., Gessner, M., & Esposito, A. Language without communication: A case study. *Journal of Child Language*. 1979, *6*, 329-352.

Bloom, L. *Learning to talk: It isn't as easy as it sounds*. Keynote Address, Annual Meeting of the Orton Society, Indianapolis, Ind., November, 1979.

Bloom, L. & Lahey, M. *Language development and language disorders*. New York: Wiley, 1978.

Brown, R. *A first language: The early stages*. Cambridge, Mass.: Harvard University Press, 1973.

Bryan, T., Donahue, M., & Pearl, R. Learning disabled children's peer interactions during a small-group problem-solving task. *Learning Disability Quarterly*, 1981a, *4*, 13-22.

Bryan, T., Donahue, M., & Pearl, R. Studies of learning disabled children's pragmatic competence. *Topics in Learning & Learning Disabilities*, 1981b, *1*, 29-39.

Bush, W., & Waugh, K. *Diagnosing learning disabilities* (2nd ed.). Columbus, O.: Charles E. Merrill, 1976.

Chassan, J. Stochastic models of the single case as the bases of clinical research design. *Behavioral Science*, 1961, *6*,42-50.

Clark, H., Carpenter, P., & Just, M. On the meeting of sematics and perception. In W. Chase (Ed.), *Visual information processing*. New York: Academic Press, 1973.

Colarusso, R., & Hammill, D. *Motor-Free Test of Visual Perception*. San Rafael, Calif.: Academic Therapy, 1972.

Coleman, H. Visual perception and reading dysfunction. *Journal of Learning Disabilities*, 1968, *1*, 116-123.

Cruickshank, W. (Ed.). *The teacher of brain-injured children: A discussion of the bases for competency*. Syracuse: Syracuse University Press, 1966.

Cruickshank, W. *Learning disabilities in home, school, and community*. Syracuse: Syracuse University Press, 1977.

Cruickshank, W., Bentzen, F., Ratzeburg, F., & Tannhauser, M. *Teaching method for brain-injured and hyperactive children*. Syracuse: Syracuse University Press, 1961.

Davol, S., & Hastings, M. Effects of sex, age, reading ability, SES, and display position on measures of spatial relationships of children. *Perceptual and Motor Skills*, 1967, *24*, 375-387.

Donahue, M., Pearl, R., & Bryan, T. Learning disabled children's conversational competence: Responses to inadequate messages. *Applied Psycholinguistics*, 1980, *1*, 387-403.

Donahue, M. Requesting strategies of learning disabled children. *Applied Psycholinguistics*, 1981, *2*, 213-234.

Dunn, L. *Peabody Picture Vocabulary Test*. Circle Pines, Minn.: American Guidance Service, 1965.

Flynn, P., & Bryne, M. Relationship between reading and selected auditory abilities of third grade children. *Journal of Speech and Hearing Research*, 1970, *13*, 731-740.

Frostig, M., & Maslow, P. Visual perception and early education. In L. Tarnopol (Ed.), *Learning disabilities: Introduction to educational and medical management*. Springfield, Ill.: Charles C. Thomas, 1969.

Gallagher, T. *Conversational analysis*. Paper presented at the North Dakota Speech and Hearing Association Convention, October, 1978.

Gallagher, T., & Darnton, B. Conversational aspects of the speech of language-disordered children: Revision behaviors. *Journal of Speech and Hearing Research*, 1978, *21*, 118-135.

Golden, N., & Steiner, S. Auditory and visual functions in good and poor readers. *Journal of Learning Disabilities*, 1969, 2, 476-481.

Guralnick, M. The application of single-subject research designs to the field of learning disabilities. *Journal of Learning Disabilities*, 1978, *11*(7), 24-30.

Hallahan, D. Comparative research studies on the psychological characteristics of learning disabled children. In W. Cruickshank & D. Hallahan (Eds.), *Perceptual and learning disabilities in children, Vol. 1: Psychoeducational practices*. Syracuse: Syracuse University Press, 1975.

Hallahan, D. Issues in special education: Rarely a case of "either-or". *Journal of Learning Disabilities*, 1977, *10*, 540-543.

Hallahan, D., & Kauffman, J. *Exceptional children: Introduction to special education*. Englewood Cliffs, N.J.: Prentice-Hall, 1978.

Hersen, M., & Barlow, D. *Single case experimental designs: Strategies for studying behavior change*. New York: Pergamon Press, 1976.

Johnson, D., & Myklebust, H. *Learning disabilities: Educational principles and practices*. New York: Grune & Stratton, 1967.

Johnson, M. C. *A review of research methods in education*. Chicago: Rand McNally, 1977.

Johnson, W., Darley, F., & Spriestersbach, D. *Diagnostic methods in speech pathology*. New York: Harper & Row, 1963.

Keogh, B., Major, S., Omori, H., Gandara, P., & Reid, H. Proposed markers in learning disabilities research. *Journal of Abnormal Child Psychology*, 1980, *8*, 21-31.

Keogh, B., Major, S., Omori, H., & Reid, H. *The development and utilization of marker variables for research in learning disabilities*. Paper presented at the Association for Children and Adults with Learning Disabilities Conference, Milwaukee, Wisc., February, 1980.

Keogh, B., Major, S., Reid, H., Gandara, P., Omori, H. Marker variables: A search for comparability and generalizability in the field of learning disabilities. *Learning Disability Quarterly*, 1978, *1*, 5-11.

Kirk, S., McCarthy, J., Kirk, W. *Illinois Test of Psycholinguistic Abilities* (Rev. ed.). Urbana, Ill.: University of Illinois Press, 1968.

Kratochwill, T. (Ed.). *Single subject research: Strategies for evaluating change*. New York: Academic Press, 1978.

Kratochwill, T., Brody, G., & Piersel, W. Time-series research: Some comments on design methodology for research in learning disabilities. *Journal of Learning Disabilities*, 1979, *12*, 257-263.

Leton, D. Visual-motor capacities and ocular efficiency in reading. *Perceptual and Motor Skills*, 1962, *15*, 406-432.

Lingren, R. Performance of disabled and normal readers on the Bender-Gestalt, Auditory Discrimination Test, and Visual-Motor Matching. *Perceptual and Motor Skills*, 1969, *29*, 152-154.

Lyle, J. Reading retardation and reversal tendency: A factorial study. *Child Development*, 1968, *40*, 833-843.

Mann, L., Goodman, L., & Wiederholt, J. (Eds.). *Teaching the learning disabled adolescent*. Boston: Houghton Mifflin, 1978.

Mercer, C. *Children and adolescents with learning disabilities*. Columbus, Oh.: Charles E. Merrill, 1979.

Myklebust, H. *Auditory disorders in children: A manual for differential diagnosis*. New York: Grune & Stratton, 1954.

Naslund, R., Thorpe, L., & Lefever, D. *SRA Achievement Series Test*. Chicago: Science Research Associates, 1978.

Parker, T., Freston, C., & Drew, C. Comparison of verbal performance of normal and learning disabled children as a function of input organization. *Journal of Learning Disabilities*, 1975, *8*, 386-392.

Pirozzolo, F. *The neuropsychology of developmental reading disorders*. New York: Praeger, 1979.

Rosenthal, J. A preliminary psycholinguistic study of children with learning disabilities. *Journal of Learning Disabilities*, 1970, *3*, 391-395.

Russell, S. *The syntactic, semantic, and pragmatic oral language production of normal and learning disabled children: A single-subject approach*. Unpublished doctoral dissertation, The University of Michigan, Ann Arbor, Michigan, 1981.

Satz, P., & Morris, R. Learning disability subtypes: A review. In F. Pirozzolo & M. Wittrock (Eds.), *Neuropsychological and cognitive processes in reading*. New York: Academic Press, 1980.

Semel, E., & Wiig, E. Comprehension of syntactic structures and critical verbal elements by children with learning disabilities. *Journal of Learning Disabilities*, 1975, *8*, 53-58.

Skubic, V., & Anderson, M. The interrelationship of perceptual-motor achievement, academic achievement, and intelligence of fourth-grade children. *Journal of Learning Disabilities*, 1970, *3*, 413-420.

Smith, M. E. Grammatical errors in the speech of preschool children. *Child Development*, 1933, *4*, 183-190. Reprinted in L. Bloom (Ed.), *Readings in language development*. New York: Wiley, 1978, 31-38.

Tallal, P. Auditory perceptual factors in language and learning disabilities. In R. Knights & D. Bakker (Eds.), *The neuropsychology of learning disorders: Theoretical approaches*. Baltimore: University Park Press, 1976.

Tallal, P., & Piercy, M. Developmental aphasia: The perception of brief vowels and extended stop consonants. *Neuropsychologia*, 1975, *13*, 69-74.

Tarnopol, L. (Ed.). *Learning disabilities: Introduction to educational and medical management*. Springfield, Ill.: Charles C. Thomas, 1969.

Vogel, S. Syntactic abilities in normal and dyslexic children. *Journal of Learning Disabilities*, 1974, *7*, 103-109.

Wechsler, D. *Wechsler Intelligence Scale for Children-Revised*. New York: Psychological Corp., 1974.

Wepman, J., Cruickshank, W., Deutsch, C., Morency, A., & Strother, C. Learning disabilities. In N. Hobbs (Ed.), *Issues in the classification of children* (Vol. I). San Francisco: Jossey-Bass, 1975.

Whipple, C., & Kodman, F. A study of discrimination and perceptual learning with retarded readers. *Journal of Educational Psychology*, 1969, *60*, 1-5.

Wiederholt, J. Historical perspectives on the education of the learning disabled. In L. Mann & D. Sabatino (Eds.), *The second review of special education*. Philadelphia: JSE Press, 1974.

Wiig, E. Language and learning disabilities: Identification and evaluation. *Australian Journal of Remedial Education*, 1976, *8*(4), 4-14.

Wiig, E., & Austin, P. Visual attention and distraction in aphasic and non-aphasic children. *Perceptual and Motor Skills*, 1972, *35*, 863-866.

Wiig, E., Lapointe, C., & Semel, E. Relationships among language processing and production abilities of learning disabled adolescents. *Journal of Learning Disabilities*, 1977, *10*, 292-299.

Wiig, E., & Roach, M. Immediate recall of semantically varied 'sentences' by learning-disabled adolescents. *Perceptual and Motor Skills*, 1975, *40*, 119-125.

Wiig, E., & Semel, E. Comprehension of linguistic concepts requiring logical operations by learning-disabled children. *Journal of Speech and Hearing Research*, 1973, *16*, 627-636.

Wiig, E., & Semel, E. Logico-grammatical sentence comprehension by adolescents with learning disabilities. *Perceptual and Motor Skills*, 1974, *38*, 1331-1334.

Wiig, E., & Semel, E. Productive language abilities in learning disabled adolescents. *Journal of Learning Disabilities*, 1975, *8*, 578-586.

Wiig, E., Semel, E., & Crouse, M. The use of English morphology by high-risk and learning disabled children. *Journal of Learning Disabilities*, 1973, *6*, 457-465.

Woodcock, R., & Johnson, M. *Woodcock-Johnson Psycho-Educational Battery*. Boston: Teaching Resources Corp., 1977.

2

Effects of Presentation Rate and Consequences
on Immediate and Long-Term Recall
of Learning Disabled Students
A Combination Multiple Baseline, Time-Series
Analyses of Single-Subject Data

Jane Y. Murdock and Laurie D. Sabrio

PROBLEMS RELATED to identifying, treating and educating learning disabled students continue to plague parents and professionals. This may be due, in part, to how we have defined learning disabilities. Since the early 1960's there have been many definitions. That of the National Advisory Committee on Handicapped Children (1968) has been one of the most influential and was changed only slightly for inclusion in Public Law 94-142, the Education for All Handicapped Children Act. Reference to an inability to understand and use language is basic to most of the definitions. Many, including the current definition in PL 94-142, make specific reference to such conditions as perceptual handicaps, brain injury, minimal brain dysfunction, dyslexia, and developmental aphasia as being included in learning disabilities.

As a result of these definitions, much of early and present work in the field of learning disabilities has focused on arranging specific antecedent and other environmental stimuli in such a way that brain damaged or minimally brain damaged students could attend to, receive, and process relevant stimuli selectively (Chalfant and Scheffelin 1969; Cruickshank 1976; Hallahan and Cruickshank 1973; Johnson and Myklebust 1967; Kephart 1960; Kirk and Gallagher 1979; Strauss and Lehtinen 1947).

There is evidence that the inability of learning disabled students to attend to incoming stimuli selectively may be the common denominator among the behavioral characteristics most often attributed to them (Ross 1976). However, much of the literature supporting this theory has investigated learning disabled subjects' ability to attend to visual as opposed to auditory stimuli. Of the 21

Special thanks to Stephen A. Zinkgraf for his assistance with the time-series analyses, to Deby Smith for serving as an independent judge, and to the children who participated. This research was funded in part through an organized research grant from the College of Education at the University of New Orleans.

studies related to attentional deficits and LD children reviewed by Tarver and Hallahan (1974), approximately 62 percent of them appeared to look at visual attention exclusively, as opposed to 14 percent that were exclusive to auditory attention. Gerber (1980) has suggested that auditory processing deficits are more likely to be the underlying problems of language or learning disabilities. Since that 1974 review, the major thrust of research related to attentional deficits in learning disabled populations has continued to focus on visual attending. Much of it used Hagen's (1967) central-incidental task, which is a visual task, as the criterion. Although limited to the visual modality, the findings suggest that learning disabled subjects experience attentional deficits and that they lag about two years behind normal children in the development of selective attention (Diekel and Friedman 1976; Druker and Hagen 1969; Hallahan, Kauffman, and Ball 1974; Tarver, Hallahan, Cohen, and Kauffman 1977).

There is an assumption that this is the result of central processing deficits experienced by the learning disabled population which corresponds with Cruickshank's (1971) definition of distractibility as being the inability to filter out extraneous stimuli and focus selectively on the task. This lead to intervention programs which reduced extraneous sensory input to a minimum in order to enable the LD or hyperactive student to focus on the academic stimuli being presented (Cruickshank, Bentzen, Ratzeburg, and Tannhauser 1961). However, it was generally concluded that such sensory restriction was not feasible in most educational settings and could be used only in conjunction with other strong academic programs (Hallahan and Cruickshank 1973).

Still considering antecedent stimuli that effect auditory attention and memory, there are some that may be more amenable to use in typical educational settings. It seems to be generally accepted that children with auditory processing difficulties should be able to attend, retrieve and recall information better when spoken material is presented at a slower rate. Wiig and Semel (1976, 1980) recommended controlling presentation rate by reducing it initially and gradually increasing the rate until it approaches that of normal speech. However, investigations of rate as it effects auditory attention and memory in learning disabled populations are inconclusive. Furthermore, few investigations looked at the effects of varying presentation rates on the overall ability of LD individuals to attend to auditory material and then retrieve and recall relevant information rather than repeat *verbatim* the digits or words they had listened to. Wiig and Semel (1980) suggest that learning disabled children and adolescents may have short-term memory deficits that show up in limited ability to repeat digits, words or phrases without having a deficit in their ability to hang onto and recall the underlying meaning of phrases and sentences. Without negating the importance of immediate sequential memory, the student's task is more often one of being able to attend to, store and retrieve, and use information appropriately that is related to the underlying meaning. We found two investigations that used rate as an independent variable to determine its effect on the ability of language or learning disabled subjects to recall underlying meaning.

McCroskey and Thompson (1973) found no significant differences in learning disabled subjects' ability to listen to material presented at five different rates measured in syllables spoken per second (2.3 sps, 2.9 sps, 3.6 sps, 5.0 sps and 6.8 sps) when data from all 20 subjects, ranging in age from 5 yr 1 mo to 16 yr 9 mo, were pooled. However, when the data for the 10 younger subjects, ranging in age from 5 yr 1 mo to 10 yr 3 mo, were separated from the older subjects, the data revealed that the young subjects comprehended material significantly better when it was presented at 2.9 sps as opposed to 5.0 sps or faster. No mention was made regarding performance at 2.3 sps or 3.6 sps, which was considered to be the normal rate.

Blosser, Weidner, and Dinero (1976) presented material at four different presentation rates (2.5 sps, 3.4 sps, 4.2 sps and 5.0 sps, which was considered the normal rate for this investigation) to children ranging in age from 5 yr 5 mo to 8 yr 0 mo. They found that normal females improved their performance as the rate of speech decreased. The same was not true for normal males. They responded better to the 4.2 sps rate than to the 3.4 sps rate. Females with language disorders responded much better to material presented at 3.4 sps and 4.2 sps than to material presented at 5.0 sps, but their performance declined slightly when the presentation rate was 2.5 sps. Males with language disorders responded much better when the rates were 2.5 sps and 3.4 sps compared to the normal rate of 5.0 sps; however, this was not true at 4.2 sps.

This variability may have been dependent upon age, sex, and language or learning disability, as the researchers suggested. Or it may be that even within one small, well identified population, e.g., young, learning disabled females, identified as having specific auditory deficits, there still would be considerable individual variability. Furthermore, these investigations required extensive electro-mechanical equipment to control presentation rates. They were also limited to responses made immediately after listening to the material. One of the questions raised is how slow is the optimum rate, i.e., one slow enough to permit brain damaged or perceptually handicapped children to process the information without being so slow that it overtaxes their memory capacity. Another question relates to what effect presentation rate might have on long-term recall, such as 24 hours later.

There appears to be minimal information related to varying consequent stimuli in order to improve attentional deficits with the learning disabled population. This may be a result of the assumption that these are central processing deficits resulting from brain damage or minimal brain damage and that, as such, would not be amenable to such simplistic solutions. However, Ayllon, Layman, and Kandel (1975) successfully reduced hyperactivity in three children diagnosed as being chronically hyperactive simply by reinforcing appropriate academic behaviors. Zlutnick, Mayville, and Moffat (1975) went a step further and used consequent stimuli to modify seizure behaviors in four subjects who each had a formal diagnosis of epilepsy based upon EEG and/or clinical observation by a certified neurologist and one subject who did not meet these medical criteria but who was alternately diagnosed as autistic, brain damaged, and as having a learning disability, and who exhibited an average of twelve seizures per day in spite of taking eight 1/4 grain tablets of Dilantin per day.

There is some literature related specifically to applying consequent stimuli in an attempt to modify attentional deficits of learning disabled subjects. Hallahan, Tarver, Kaufman, and Graybeal (1978) found that delivering tangible reinforcers improved visual sequential memory of 7- to 14-yr-old LD subjects. The authors contributed these results to the motivating effect the consequences had on attending behaviors. However, Dawson (1978) found that reinforcement did not significantly increase a group of 9-yr-old and a group of 11-yr-old learning disabled students' ability to attend to a visual task. In fact, Dawson speculated that reinforcement may have raised the subjects' anxiety level to such a degree that it interfered with their ability to recall visual sequential material.

It is possible that much of the contradictory findings in the foregoing literature related to learning disabled subjects resulted from the heterogeneity of the population that is labeled "learning disabled." A subject may be identified as learning disabled but may have auditory as opposed to visual processing deficits, or vice versa, or may have no processing deficits, but simply be distractible or hyperactive. There is an assumption in traditional statistical research procedures that the results cannot possibly go beyond the sampling procedures used. It is obvious that random sampling procedures are necessarily limited when we are looking at populations that, by definition, are exceptional and that are also heterogeneous. If, for example, two groups of learning disabled students were randomly selected, and one was to receive some reinforcing consequences for attending to auditory stimuli and one was not, there is an assumption that the groups are equal, i.e., the random selection allowed for an experimental group and a matched control group. Unless these students were specifically described as having comparable auditory processing abilities (or disabilities), one might anticipate contradictory findings with research replications, since it is very possible that random assignment in a small, heterogeneous population could easily result in noncomparable groups, at least occasionally. Guralnick (1978) suggested that single-subject research designs would overcome this problem. When a subject serves as his/her own control, you should have a perfectly matched control. Furthermore, such designs lend themselves to much needed individual data that are lost in the group means of traditional research designs.

This is not to conclude that single-subject research designs are without problems. DeProspero and Cohen (1979) found that the visual inferences drawn by a panel of judges, who simply looked at graphs used to report single-subject data, were not as reliable as statistical inferences drawn from the same data. Hartmann, Gottman, Jones, Gardner, Kazdin and Vaught (1980) suggested that a time-series or interrupted time-series analysis should be applied to single-subject data whenever serial dependency or variability might be present.

In view of the above, there appears to be a need for research related specifically to auditory attention and consequent ability to respond correctly in learning disabled subjects. It should include investigating both antecedent and consequent stimuli. It should look at long-term as well as immediate responding. Ideally, it should use young subjects since previous research suggests that attentional problems may be overcome by adolescence. The subjects should be specifically diagnosed as having auditory attention and/or memory deficits. While applied research done by psychologists, speech therapists and other professionals is invaluable, in order to encourage generalization from research to practice, the research should be conducted by an on-site teacher in a fairly typical school setting. A single-subject research design that includes time-series analyses should be used to help to overcome many of the problems mentioned related to both traditional and single-subject research designs when used with a learning disabled population. It is the purpose of the present investigation to address these problems.

METHOD

Subjects and Setting

The subjects were all white females, enrolled in the same self-contained LD classroom in the New Orleans metropolitan area. Pseudonyms have been assigned to each to protect their identity. Specific information is given on each subject that is relevant to her auditory attention or memory deficits.

Marie was 9 yr 2 mo of age when she was tested at the beginning of this study. She had a full-scale WISC-R score of 70. Her poorest subtest performance on the WISC-R was Digit Span. Her age score was lower than 3 yr 0 mo for the Auditory Attention Unrelated Words subtest and 4 yr 3 mo for the Auditory Attention Related Syllables subtest of the *Detroit Tests for Learning Aptitude*. On the *Illinois Test of Psycholinguistic Abilities*, her age scores for the auditory channel were consistently lower than those for the visual channel, except for Auditory Reception. Her specific Auditory Memory age score was 4 yr 0 mo, which was a full year lower than any other subtest score.

Diane was 8 yr 6 mo of age when she was tested at the beginning of this study. She had a full-scale WISC-R score of 84. Her poorest subtest performance on the WISC-R was Digit Span. Her age score was 3 yr 3 mo for Auditory Attention Unrelated Words and 4 yr 0 mo for Auditory Attention Related Syllables subtests of the *Detroit Tests for Learning Aptitude*. On the *Illinois Test for Psycholinguistic Abilities*, her age scores for the auditory channel were consistently lower than those for the visual channel, except for Auditory Reception. Her specific Auditory Memory age score was 5 yr 3 mo, which was lower than any other score except 4 yr 0 mo for Grammatic Closure.

Karen was 8 yr 7 mo of age when she was tested at the beginning of this study. She had a full-scale WISC-R score of 68. Her lowest subtest score on the WISC-R was Digit Span. Her age score was lower than 3 yr 0 mo for the Auditory Attention Unrelated Words subtest and 3 yr 9 mo for the Auditory Attention Related Syllables subtest ofthe *Detroit Tests for Learning Aptitude*. On the *Illinois Test of Psycholinguistic Abilities*, her age scores ranged from low scores of 3 yr 1 mo and 3 yr 5 mo for Visual Memory and Auditory Memory, respectively, to high scores of 7 yr 0 mo for both Auditory Association and Auditory Reception. By definition, a learning disabled student in the State of Louisiana must have an IQ of 70 or above. However, in borderline cases, other factors may be taken into consideration. It is interesting that Karen had a full-scale IQ score of 68 when she was tested for the purposes of this investigation, but had a full-scale score of 79 a year and a half earlier.

The setting was a conference room in the school which contained a large conference table, six chairs, a filing cabinet, a variety of portable supplies that various school personnel would leave in the room, plus the video equipment used in this investigation. There was also a floor-to-ceiling window that overlooked the playground. There was considerable traffic and talking outside the window, as well as in the hallway. There was no attempt to alter or minimize visual or auditory stimuli typical to a school setting, except that the secretary was asked to shut off the intercommunication speaker in that room while we were recording data. She usually remembered to do so. The second investigator, who was the subjects' teacher at the time these data were collected, worked directly with the students in this conference room where they had been tutored frequently in the past. Video recording equipment was set up in advance and every session was videotaped.

Design

The data were collected using a multiple baseline procedure (Baer, Wolf, and Risley 1968) across four different conditions. The conditions were (1) responding immediately to 10 questions based on material presented at a rate of

2.0 sps, (2) responding on the next school day to the same 10 questions, (3) responding immediately to 10 questions based on material presented at a rate of 3.5 sps, and (4) responding on the next school day to the same 10 questions. After baseline measures (Baseline) were taken, social consequences (Socials) were introduced sequentially across the four conditions and presented following correct responses. During the final phase of the investigation, tangible consequences (Tangibles) were paired with the social consequences and were introduced sequentially across the four conditions contingent upon correct responding.

To analyze the multiple baseline data, time-series analyses using multiple regression were used to model the Baseline, Socials, and Tangibles responses over trials. A dummy variable (i.e., 0's and 1's) was created for each phase (Wesolowsky 1976). The dummy variable to represent the Socials phase was assigned the value of unity if the response occurred within that phase and zero if the response occurred within the Baseline or Tangibles phase. Likewise, the dummy variable that represented the Tangibles phase was assigned the value of unity if the response occurred within that phase and zero if the response occurred within the Baseline or Socials phase. Using this approach, the regression constant represented the mean for the baseline responses, and the regression weights for each of the dummy variables represented the response increment above or below baseline for the respective phases. The regression weights for each phase were tested for statistical significance using ordinary least squares methodology. Before these tests were performed, however, the independence of the regression residuals was tested using the Durbin-Watson statistic.

Reliability

Since the data for this study were collected in a natural setting and were observational in nature, the reliability of the data collection procedures was critical (Hartmann 1977). Furthermore, the teaching procedures were carefully controlled in order to ascertain that presentation rates were accurate and that the teacher-investigator reliably presented consequences (Murdock, Garcia, and Hardman 1977). In order to control for these two essential conditions, it was necessary to videotape every session throughout the duration of the study so that two judges could observe independently (1) whether the students' verbal responses were correct or incorrect, (2) whether the teacher-investigator's presentation rates were accurate within plus or minus .25 sps, and (3) whether and what kind of consequences were presented.

Only those responses that the two independent judges agreed upon as being correct were scored as correct and used in this study. Consequently, whenever the judges disagreed, or agreed that a response was incorrect, the

response was considered as an incorrect response and was so scored. The reliability of these data was 99.7 percent, calculated by dividing the number of
agreements by the number of agreements plus disagreements and multiplying
that figure by 100. If the judges did not agree that the presentation rate was
accurate within plus or minus .25 sps, the data collected during those sessions
were discarded. At no time during this study did either of the judges determine
that the teacher-investigator delivered consequences inappropriately.

Procedures

The multiple baseline procedure involved first collecting baseline data on
all of the subjects and then sequentially applying the intervention procedures to
each subject in each of the four listening conditions (Baer, Wolf, and Risley
1968). Each subject answered questions immediately and on the next school
day after having listened to material spoken at two different rates. First, the
subjects received no consequences (Baseline), then social consequences (Socials) and finally social plus tangible consequences (Tangibles) were presented
following correct responses. These consequences were sequentially introduced
in the four different conditions: (1) immediate responding to material read at
2.0 sps, (2) next-school-day responding to the same material, (3) immediate
responding to material read at 3.5 sps, and (4) next-school-day responding to
the same material. The order of the sequential treatment across these conditions
varied from subject to subject, making certain that in at least one phase of the
study each of the subjects received consequences for responding correctly on
the next school day, when she had not received any consequences for responding correctly immediately after listening to the material. The purpose of this
was to attempt to isolate the motivating effects of the consequences, uncon-
taminated by prior modeling and reinforcing consequences.

One hundred reading passages were prepared in advance to be used in this
investigation, two for each of the 50 data points. Each story consisted of 10
simple sentences that were related to each other so as to tell a complete inci-
dent. Vocabulary and syntax were controlled so that neither exceeded the
second grade reading level. The stories were randomly assigned to one of the
two rate conditions for each student. Ten questions were written for each of
the story incidents, one for each sentence. The questions were who, what,
when or how questions which did not require any operations beyond simple,
convergent production.

Each of the two randomly assigned stories corresponded to vertically
related data points on the multiple baseline graphic presentations of the data.
This was to control for the almost inevitable differences in interest level and
question difficulty. The intrasubject multiple baseline data reflected each sub-

ject's responses to two different randomly selected stories, one she had listened to at 2.0 sps and one she had listened to at 3.5 sps. Replication across subjects was done in such a way that one subject may have been listening to a story at 2.0 sps with social consequences, while another was listening to the same story at 3.5 sps with no consequences, and another at 3.5 sps with social or tangible consequences.

The rate at which the material was read was determined by calculating the number of syllables read per second. The specific rates of 2.0 sps and 3.5 sps were selected as an extension of a pilot study in which 3.5 sps had been both the slowest and the optimum rate. The present investigation extended it even further to 2.0 sps in an attempt to determine how slow the optimum rate might be for young learning disabled females to process auditory material (Blosser et al. 1976; McCroskey and Thompson 1973) without having adverse effects on memory. The teacher-investigator who collected the data practiced reading at 3.5 and 2.0 sps prior to this investigation. She also practiced each specified rate for the reading samples to be read immediately prior to each data collection session until she could read the 10-sentence passages at the correct rates (plus or minus .25 sps) at least once, or as many readings as it took for her "to have a feeling" for the pacing. Two independent judges listened to videotapes of each data collection session and timed the reading rates before recording any of the data. If the rates were not within plus or minus .25 sps of the specified limits of 3.5 sps and 2.0 sps, those data were not used in this study.

During Baseline each subject was instructed to listen carefully in order to be able to answer some questions. The teacher-investigator then asked the subject ten questions. She did not provide any feedback. She did not even look at the subject following responses because we felt that this might contaminate the Socials phase of the investigation (Murdock et al. 1977).

The Socials phase consisted of the same instructions and questioning procedures as during Baseline, plus eye contact, verbal praise and smiling for correct answers and correcting incorrect responses by saying, "Not quite, . . . " and telling the student the correct answer. The Tangibles phase consisted of the same instructions and questioning procedures, plus calling the student's attention to placing a plus mark on a score sheet whenever she responded correctly, in addition to the social consequences. The student could then select one, two or three edible rewards at the end of the session, depending upon the number of pluses earned. A situation was created that would avoid reducing the possible motivating effect of the tangible rewards by telling the student that she could buy one edible for five pluses, two edibles for more than five pluses, and three edibles if all ten questions were answered correctly. The edibles were small boxes of raisins and various kinds of candy.

During each of the above phases, the data collected were the 10 questions asked immediately after each of the two readings and the same questions asked again on the following school day. In other words, each subject was asked 10 questions on each story she had listened to yesterday and 10 questions on each of the current stories, for a total of 40 questions each day.

RESULTS

While responding was consistently better for all three subjects when material was presented at 3.5 sps as compared to 2.0 sps, these differences were not statistically significant at the .05 level of confidence. The data revealed that all of the subjects responded significantly better when they received tangible consequences regardless of the presentation rate. The possibility of the results being due to serial dependency was minimized by applying the Durbin-Watson test for significance. The individual results follow.

Marie

The multiple baseline conditions for Marie were presented in the following order: First, next-school-day responding to material presented at 2.0 sps. Second, immediate responding to material presented at 2.0 sps. Third, next-school-day responding to material presented at 3.5 sps. Finally, immediate responding to material presented at 3.5 sps. Refer to Figure 1 for a presentation of Marie's multiple baseline data and Table 1 for the mean number of correct responses made during each of the three phases across the four different conditions contrasted with the time-series analyses of the same data.

The data revealed that Marie had a mean of 3.80 correct responses during baseline when she was answering questions the next school day on material she had listened to at 2.0 sps. Her performance increased to a mean of 5.50 (F calculated = 2.57) when she received social consequences for correct responding which was not statistically significant. When Marie received tangible consequences for correct responding, her performance increased to a mean of 7.26 (F calculated = 13.97) which was statistically significant beyond the .01 level of confidence.

During the second condition when Marie was responding immediately to material she had listened to at 2.0 sps, she had a mean of 5.13 correct responses

Figure 2.1.   Marie's multiple baseline data. Each data point represents the number of correct responses out of a possible 10 on questions asked either immediately after listening to a story or on the following school day. Two different stories are involved: one read at 2.0 sps and one read at 3.5 sps.

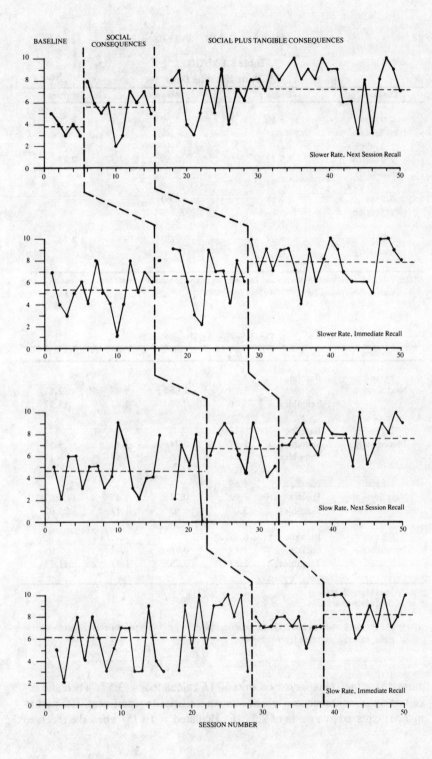

Table 2.1 MARIE
Multiple Baseline Data

Condition	Baseline	Socials	Tangibles
2.0 sps Next Session	3.80	5.50	7.26
2.0 sps Immediately	5.13	6.50	7.77
3.5 sps Next Session	4.68	6.60	7.77
3.5 sps Immediately	6.07	7.20	8.58

NOTE: Figures Under Baseline, Socials and Tangibles represent the mean number of correct responses during each of those phases for each of the four conditions.

Time-Series Analyses

Condition	Phase	B	SE	DF	F
2.0 sps Next Session	Baseline Socials Tangibles	3.80 1.70 3.46	 1.06 0.93	 1,47 1,47	 2.57 13.97†
2.0 sps Immediately	Baseline Socials Tangibles	5.13 1.37 2.64	 0.74 0.66	 1,47 1,47	 3.57 16.15†
3.5 sps Next Session	Baseline Socials Tangibles	4.68 1.92 3.09	 0.74 0.62	 1,47 1,47	 6.67* 25.02†
3.5 sps Immediately	Baseline Socials Tangibles	6.07 1.13 2.51	 0.78 0.73	 1,47 1,47	 2.08 11.73†

* < .05 level of significance
† < .01 level of significance

NOTE: The B value for Socials and Tangibles represents the mean gain over mean Baseline values for each of those phases in each of the four conditions.

during baseline. This increased to 6.50 (F calculated $= 3.57$) when she received social consequences which was not statistically significant. Her performance increased to a mean of 7.77 (F calculated $= 16.15$) when she received both social and tangible consequences which was statistically significant beyond the .01 level of confidence.

In the third condition when Marie was responding to the 10 questions on material presented at 3.5 sps on the following school day, she had a mean of 4.68 correct responses during baseline. This increased to 6.60 (F calculated = 6.67) when she received social consequences which was statistically significant beyond the .05 level of confidence. Her performance further increased to a mean of 7.77 (F calculated = 25.02) when she was receiving both social and tangible consequences which was statistically significant beyond the .01 level of confidence.

In the final condition when Marie was responding immediately to material read at 3.5 sps, she had a mean of 6.07 correct responses during baseline. This increased to 7.20 (F calculated = 2.08) when she received social consequences which was not statistically significant. Her performance further increased to a mean of 8.58 (F calculated = 11.73) when she received tangible consequences which was statistically significant beyond the .01 level of confidence.

Diane

The multiple baseline conditions for Diane were presented in the following order: First, immediate responding at 3.5 sps. Second, next-school-day responding at 2.0 sps. Third, immediate responding at 2.0 sps. Finally, next-school-day responding at 3.5 sps. Refer to Figure 2 for a visual presentation of Diane's multiple baseline data and Table 2 for the mean number of correct responses during each of the three phases for each of the four multiple baseline conditions contrasted with the time-series analyses of the same data.

The data revealed that Diane had a mean of 5.00 correct responses when answering 10 questions immediately on material presented at 3.5 sps. This dropped to a mean of 4.55 (F calculated = 0.29) when she received social consequences for correct responses which was not statistically significant. Diane's performance increased to a mean of 6.88 (F calculated = 4.31) when she received tangible consequences which was statistically significant beyond the .05 level of confidence.

In the second condition of answering 10 questions on the following school day to material presented at 2.0 sps, Diane had a mean of 4.92 correct responses during baseline. This increased to a mean of 5.77 (F calculated = 0.34) when she received social consequences which was not statistically significant. Her performance increased to a mean of 8.29 (F calculated = 37.86) when she received social plus tangible consequences which was statistically significant beyond the .01 level of confidence.

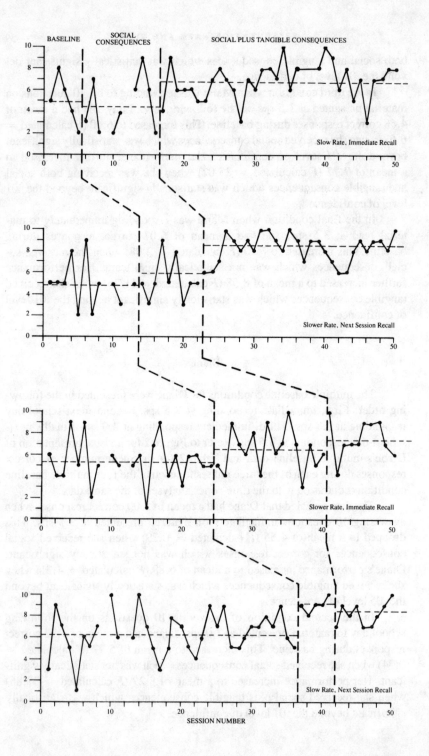

Table 2.2 DIANE
Multiple Baseline Data

Condition	Baseline	Socials	Tangibles
3.5 sps Immediately	5.00	4.55	6.88
2.0 sps Next Session	4.92	5.77	8.29
2.0 sps Immediately	5.33	6.44	7.50
3.5 sps Next Session	6.31	9.00	8.22

NOTE: Figures Under Baseline, Socials and Tangibles represent the mean number of correct responses during each of those phases for each of the four conditions.

Time-Series Analyses

Condition	Phase	B	SE	DF	F
3.5 sps Immediately	Baseline	5.00			
	Socials	-0.45	1.03	1,47	0.29
	Tangibles	1.88	0.91	1,47	4.31†
2.0 sps Next Session	Baseline	4.92			
	Socials	0.85	0.71	1,47	0.34
	Tangibles	3.37	0.55	1,47	37.86†
2.0 sps Immediately	Baseline	5.33			
	Socials	1.10	0.62	1,47	3.17
	Tangibles	2.17	0.72	1,47	8.96†
3.5 sps Next Session	Baseline	6.31			
	Socials	2.69	0.84	1,47	10.18†
	Tangibles	1.91	0.66	1,47	8.45†

* < .05 level of significance
† < .01 level of significance

NOTE: The *B* value for Socials and Tangibles represents the mean gain or loss as compared to the mean baseline values for each of those phases in each of the four conditions.

Figure 2.2. Diane's multiple baseline data. Each data point represents the number of correct responses out of a possible 10 on questions asked either immediately after listening to a story or on the following school day. Two different stories are involved: one read at 2.0 sps and one read at 3.5 sps.

During the third condition when Diane was responding to 10 questions immediately after listening to material read to her at 2.0 sps, she had a mean of 5.33 correct responses during baseline. This increased to 6.44 (F calculated = 3.17) which was not statistically significant. There was an increase to 7.50 (F calculated = 8.96) when she received social plus tangible consequences for correct responses which was statistically significant beyond the .01 level of confidence.

In the final condition when Diane was responding to the 10 questions the following school day on material that had been read to her at 3.5 sps, she responded correctly with a mean of 6.3 during baseline. This increased to a mean of 9.0 (F calculated = 10.18) when she was receiving social consequences and to a mean of 8.2 (F calculated = 8.45) when she was receiving social plus tangible consequences for correct responding. Both of these phases were statistically significant beyond the .01 level of confidence when compared to baseline performance.

Karen

The multiple baseline conditions were presented in the following order for Karen: First, immediate responding at 2.0 sps. Second, next-school-day responding at 2.0 sps. Third, next-school-day responding at 3.5 sps. Finally, immediate responding at 3.5 sps. Refer to Figure 2.3 for a visual presentation of Karen's multiple baseline data and Table 2.3 for the mean number of correct responses during each of the three phases for each of the four multiple baseline conditions contrasted with the time-series analyses of the same data.

The data revealed that Karen responded correctly at a mean of 5.50 during baseline when answering 10 questions immediately after listening to material read to her at 2.0 sps. This increased to a mean of 6.33 (F calculated = 0.86) when she received social consequences for correct responses which was not statistically significant. When she received tangible consequences, her performance increased to a mean of 8.26 (F calculated = 18.45) which was statistically significant beyond the .01 level of confidence.

During the second condition when Karen was answering questions on the following school day to material she had listened to at 2.0 sps, she responded

Figure 2.3. Karen's multiple baseline data. Each data point represents the number of correct responses out of a possible 10 on questions asked either immediately after listening to a story or on the following school day. Two different stories are involved: one read at 2.0 sps and one read at 3.5 sps.

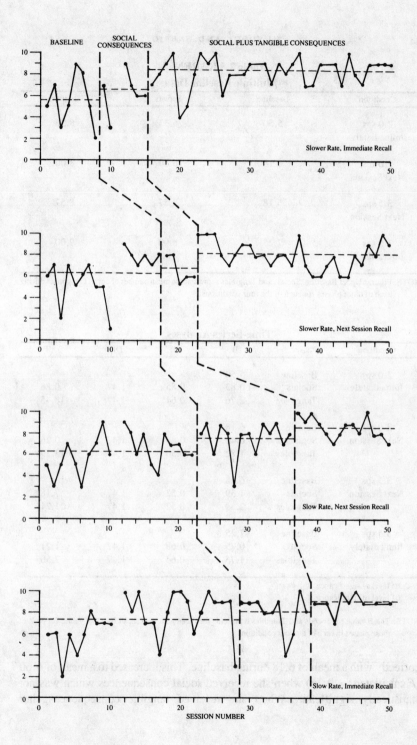

BASELINE SOCIAL CONSEQUENCES SOCIAL PLUS TANGIBLE CONSEQUENCES

Slower Rate, Immediate Recall

Slower Rate, Next Session Recall

Slow Rate, Next Session Recall

Slow Rate, Immediate Recall

SESSION NUMBER

MURDOCK AND SABRIO

Table 2.3 KAREN
Multiple Baseline Data

Condition	Baseline	Socials	Tangibles
2.0 sps Immediately	5.50	6.33	8.26
2.0 sps Next Session	6.18	6.60	8.00
3.5 sps Next Session	6.18	7.57	8.57
3.5 sps Immediately	7.25	8.00	9.00

NOTE: Figures Under Baseline, Socials and Tangibles represent the mean number of correct responses during each of those phases for each of the four conditions.

Time-Series Analyses

Condition	Phase	B	SE	DF	F
2.0 sps Immediately	Baseline	5.50			
	Socials	0.83	0.85	1,47	0.86
	Tangibles	2.76	0.64	1,47	18.45†
2.0 sps Next Session	Baseline	6.18			
	Socials	0.42	0.83	1,47	0.26
	Tangibles	1.82	0.50	1,47	13.39†
3.5 sps Next Session	Baseline	6.18			
	Socials	1.39	0.52	1,47	7.18*
	Tangibles	2.39	0.52	1,47	21.24†
3.5 sps Immediately	Baseline	7.25			
	Socials	0.75	0.68	1,47	1.21
	Tangibles	1.75	0.64	1,47	7.50†

* < .05 level of significance
† < .01 level of significance

NOTE: The B value for Socials and Tangibles represents the mean gain over mean Baseline values for each of those phases in each of the four conditions.

correctly with a mean of 6.18 during baseline. This increased to a mean of 6.60 (F calculated = 0.26) when she received social consequences which was not statistically significant. When she received tangible consequences, her performance increased to a mean of 8.00 (F calculated = 13.39) which was statistically significant beyond the .01 level of confidence.

In the third condition when Karen was answering questions on the following school day in response to material she had listened to at 3.5 sps, she responded correctly with a mean of 6.18 during baseline. This increased to a mean of 7.57 (F calculated = 7.18) when she was receiving social consequences which was statistically significant beyond the .05 level of confidence. When she was receiving both social and tangible consequences, she had a mean of 8.57 (F calculated = 21.24) which was significant beyond the .01 level of confidence.

In the final condition when Karen was answering questions immediately after listening to material read to her at a rate of 3.5 sps, her mean number of correct responses during baseline was 7.25. This increased to 8.00 (F calculated = 1.21) when she received social consequences which was not statistically significant. When she received tangible consequences for correct responses she had a mean of 9.00 (F calculated = 7.50), which was statistically significant beyond the .01 level of confidence.

DISCUSSION

Young learning disabled females identified as having specific auditory attention and memory deficits did not respond significantly better when answering questions related to material read at either 3.5 sps or 2.0 sps. There was, however, a consistent trend to respond slightly better when the rate was 3.5 sps. These findings are similar to those of McCroskey and Thompson (1973) for young learning disabled subjects and Blosser, Weidner and Dinero (1976) for language disabled female subjects. Perhaps the most important finding related to presentation rate, was that an on-site teacher can vary speaking rate reliably. Furthermore, keeping individual data provided systematic feedback regarding optimum speaking rates for individual students.

Presenting consequent stimuli, particularly tangibles, significantly improved the subjects' ability to answer questions correctly both immediately and on the next school day, regardless of the presentation rate. These findings suggest that we continue to investigate very carefully the ramifications of consequences, while not ignoring the etiological implications involved. Learning disabled children may, indeed, suffer from brain damage or minimal brain damage. This may affect their ability to inhibit extraneous sensory input and thus selectively attend, receive, perceive, process and use immediately relevant sensory information as efficiently as normal children do. The educational response to this traditionally has been to try to modify incoming stimuli or competing stimuli to enhance the learning disabled person's ability to attend to and process information selectively. The present investigation concurs with the findings of Ayllon, Layman and Kandel (1975), Hallahan, Tarver, Kauffman and Graybeal (1978), and Zlutnick, Mayville and Moffat (1975) that consequent stimuli can be arranged so as to enhance responding in subjects who have, or may have, neurological involvement. It is assumed that this is the result of increasing the subjects' motivation to attend. It is also assumed that repeated pairing of the social consequences with the tangible consequences would result in their eventually assuming the same reinforcing properties as the tangibles (Skinner 1953). Thus, tangible consequences could be faded out gradually. There is some evidence that this may have been occurring with Marie and Diane as each of these subject's responding improved significantly during at least one condition when only social consequences were delivered. Future research might alternate the Socials and Tangibles phases, rather than consistently having Socials precede Tangibles as they did in this investigation.

By conducting this investigation in an actual school setting, with the subjects' teacher serving as the trainer, we hoped to increase the possibility of any positive findings generalizing to other teachers who are concerned about the attending, listening and responding behaviors of students. While these subjects were worked with individually, these or similar reinforcing procedures could be used with small groups or even classrooms. Conducting the investigation in a school setting also provided evidence that these learning disabled subjects could be motivated to attend to auditory input, and apparently process, store, and retrieve it better when they were reinforced for doing so, regardless of other visual and auditory stimuli in the environment.

The single-subject research design proved to be an extremely useful tool, not only for research purposes, but for the continuous feedback it provided. The feedback proved to be very positive for the teacher-investigator because she had evidence of the effectiveness of her instruction. For these reasons we recommend that all teachers use similar data recording procedures at least occasionally.

The time-series multiple regression analysis applied to the multiple baseline data strengthened the interpretation of the data which otherwise may have been obscured by possible autocorrelation or variability of the data. Even with the means provided, it may be difficult to interpret graphs consistently when there is considerable variation within each phase, as was present in these data, particularly during most of the Baselines and Socials phases. The data stabilized considerably for all three subjects when they were in the Tangibles phase, which is another indication of the motivating effects of the tangible consequences.

REFERENCES

Ayllon, T., D. Layman, and H. J. Kandel. "A Behavioral-Educational Alternative to Drug Control of Hyperactive Children." *Journal of Applied Behavior Analysis* 8 (1975): 137-46.

Baer, D. M., M. M.Wolf, and T. R. Risley. "Some Current Dimensions of Applied Behavior Analysis." *Journal of Applied Behavior Analysis* 1 (1968): 91-7.

Blosser, J. L., W. E. Weidner, and T. Dinero. "The Effect of Rate-Controlled Speech on the Auditory Receptive Score of Children with Normal and Disordered Language Abilities." *The Journal of Special Education* 10 (1976): 291-98.

Chalfant, J. C., and M. A. Scheffelin. *Central Processing Dysfunctions in Children.* Bethesda: National Institute of Neurological Diseases and Stroke, Monograph No. 9, 1969.

Cruickshank, W. M. "William M. Cruickshank." In J. M. Kauffman and D. P. Hallahan, eds., *Teaching Children with Learning Disabilities: Personal Perspectives.* Columbus, O.: Merrill, 1976.

Cruickshank, W. M., and J. L. Paul. "The Psychological Characteristics of Brain-Injured Children." In W. M. Cruickshank, Ed., *Psychology of Exceptional Children and Youth.* Englewood Cliffs, N.J.: Prentice-Hall, 1971.

Cruickshank, W. M., F. A. Bentzen, F. H. Ratzeburg, and M. Tannhauser. *A Teaching Method for Brain-Injured and Hyperactive Children.* Syracuse, N. Y.: Syracuse University Press, 1961.

Dawson, M. M. "The Effect of Reinforcement and Verbal Rehearsal on Selective Attention in Learning Disabled Children." Doctoral Dissertation, University of Virginia, 1978. *Dissertation Abstracts International*, 1979, 39(A)4179.

Deikel, S. M., and M. P. Friedman. "Selective Attention in Children with Learning Disabilities." *Perceptual and Motor Skills*, 42 (1976): 675-78.

DeProspero, A., and S. Cohen. "Inconsistent Visual Analyses of Intrasubject Data." *Journal of Applied Behavior Analysis* 12 (1979):573-79.

Druker, J. F., and J. W. Hagen. "Developmental Trends in the Processing of Task-Relevant and Task-Irrelevant Information." *Child Development* 40 (1969): 371-82.

Gerber, A. "Processing and Use of Language in Education." In *Language and Learning Disabilities*, edited by A. Gerber and D. N. Bryen. Baltimore: University Park Press, 1980.

Guralnick, M. J. "The Application of Single-Subject Research Designs to the Field of Learning Disabilities." *Journal of Learning Disabilities* 11 (1978):415-21.

Hagen, J. W. "The Effect of Distraction on Selective Attention." *Child Development* 38 (1967):685-94.

Hallahan, D. P., and W. M. Cruickshank. *Psychoeducational Foundations of Learning Disabilities.* Englewood Cliffs, N.J.: Prentice-Hall, 1973.

Hallahan, D. P., J.M. Kauffman, and D. W. Ball. "Selective Attention and Cognitive Tempo of Low Achieving and High Achieving Sixth Grade Males." *Perceptual and Motor Skills* 36 (1973): 579-83.

Hallahan, D. P., S. G. Tarver, J. M. Kauffman, and N. L. Graybeal. "A Comparison of the Effects of Reinforcement and Response Cost on the Selective Attention of Learning Disabled Children." *Journal of Learning Disabilities* 11 (1978): 430-38.

Hartmann, D. P. "Considerations in Choosing an Interobserver Reliability Estimate." *Journal of Applied Behavior Analysis* 10 (1977): 103-16.

Hartman, D. P., J. M. Gottman, R. R. Jones, W. Gardner, A. E. Kazdin, and R. Vaught. "Interrupted Time-Series Analysis and Its Application to Behavioral Data." *Journal of Applied Behavior Analysis* 13 (1980): 543-59.

Johnson, D., and H. Myklebust. *Learning Disabilities: Educational Principles and Practices*. New York: Grune & Stratton, 1967.

Kauffman, J. M., and D. P. Hallahan. *Teaching Children with Learning Disabilities*. Columbus, Oh.: Charles E. Merrill Publishing Company, 1976.

Kephart, N. C. *The Slow Learner in the Classroom*. Columbus, O.: Charles E. Merrill, 1960.

Kirk, S. A., and J. J. Gallagher. *Educating Exceptional Children*, 3rd ed. Boston: Houghton Mifflin, 1979.

McCroskey, R. L., and N. W. Thompson. "Comprehension of Rate Controlled Speech by Children with Specific Learning Disabilities." *Journal of Learning Disabilities* 6 (1973): 621-27.

Murdock, J. Y., E. E. Garcia, and M.L. Hardman. "Generalizing Articulation Training with Trainable Mentally Retarded Subjects." *Journal of Applied Behavior Analysis* 10 (1977): 717-33.

Ross, A. O. *Psychological Aspects of Learning Disabilities and Reading Disorders*. New York: McGraw-Hill, 1976.

Skinner, B. F. *Science and Human Behavior*. New York: Appleton-Century-Crofts, 1953.

Strauss, A., and L. Lehtinen. *Psychopathology and Education of the Brain-Injured Child*. New York: Grune & Stratton, 1947.

Tarver, S. G., and D. P. Hallahan. "Attentional Deficits in Children with Learning Disabilities: A Review." *Journal of Learning Disabilities* 7 (1974): 560-69.

Tarver, S. G., D. P. Hallahan, S. B. Cohen, and J. M. Kauffman. "The Development of Visual Selective Attention and Verbal Rehearsal in Learning Disabled Boys." *Journal of Learning Disabilities* 10 (1977): 491-500.

Tarver, S. G., D. P. Hallahan, J. M. Kauffman, and D. W. Ball. "Verbal Rehearsal and Selective Attention in Children with Learning Disabilities: A Developmental Lag." *Journal of Experimental Child Psychology* 22 (1976): 375-85.

Wesolowsky, G. O. *Multiple Regression and Analysis of Variance: An Introduction for Computer Users in Management and Economics*. New York: John Wiley, 1976.

Wiig, E. H., and E. M. Semel. *Language Disabilities in Children and Adolescents*. Columbus, O.: Charles E. Merrill, 1976.

Wiig, E. H., and E. M. Semel. *Language Assessment & Intervention*. Columbus, O.: Charles E. Merrill, 1980.

Zlutnick, S., W. J. Mayville, and S. Moffat. "Modification of Seizure Disorders: The Interruption of Behavioral Chains." *Journal of Applied Behavior Analysis* 8 (1975): 1-12.

3

Systematizing Assistance for Intermediate/Secondary Disabled Spellers

Betty H. Yarborough and Clare M. Silva

THE TEACHING OF SPELLING, according to Venezky (1980), remains today not very far advanced beyond nineteenth-century pedagogy. There is hardly a teacher in any discipline who does not recognize the importance of spelling or, more specifically, the importance of the lack of ability to spell. Yet efforts to improve spelling instruction do not compare in any measure to those designed to improve reading instruction. The professional literature is fragmented as to both the causes and possible resolutions of spelling problems, although interest in writing, particularly in remedial instruction for the writing disabled, has resulted in increased scholarship in spelling over the last decade. One outcome of this increased scholarship has been the development of several error classification schemes designed to pinpoint specific kinds of spelling errors.

Unfortunately, the error classification systems that have proceeded from research to date are of little immediate assistance to the typical writing (or spelling) teacher at the secondary or post-secondary level. The methods for analyzing spelling errors have proceeded from a variety of points of view, but they are, nevertheless, principally of academic rather than practical interest; and they are generally concerned with children's spelling. The Holmes and Peper (1977) type of analysis is probably the one most widely known. It is principally concerned with rather mechanical vowel and consonant deletion, substitution, and addition processes. Avakian-Whitaker and Whitaker (1973) posit an analysis which considers error at the letter, syllable, and word levels — but in children's writing. Cromer's schema (in Frith 1980) for analyzing children's errors as phono-graphical, visual, morphological, spelling rule, segmentation, letter forms, and unclassifiable is more sophisticated, but probably not easily used by the writing teacher, since the constraints for excluding errors from the different categories may not be readily understood. Hotopf's (also in Frith 1980) classification of errors (as sound pattern slips, stem variants, order, repetition, omission, blends, and semantic errors) proceeds from a slips-of-the-pen viewpoint that is illuminating for interpreting some kinds of error. Frith's suggested analysis (1980) — that of distinguishing phonetic from non-phonetic error — is simple but not sufficiently informative for most practical learning situations. Shaughnessy (1977) presents an admittedly rough and ready, nonsystematic classification of spelling errors in college students' writing, which includes observations regarding homophone confusion, visual memory problems, unfamiliarity with word structure, pronunciation spelling, and orthographic unpredictabilities. In general, however, none of the existing schema have met our need for a diagnostic/remedial decision-making protocol for adolescent/adult spellers.

As persons involved in the day-by-day responsibilities of diagnosing the needs of older disabled spellers and meeting these needs through appropriate remedial intervention, we have not been able to find among existing models an accompanying error classification protocol to provide specific identification of the spelling needs of our students. Accordingly, we have designed a model of spelling upon which we have developed a new error classification strategy. In doing so, we have had the following objectives:

1. to determine the frequency of given types of errors in students' writing so that specific misconceptions about English spelling can be recognized and corrected. We also believe that spelling errors should not be confused with handwriting problems, usage problems, etc.

2. to identify severely disabled spellers, a process which we do not believe can be accomplished simply on the basis of counting the number of errors in student writing. The nature of the errors themselves is the critical variable. A word with a single letter error, for example, may not represent the same intensity of spelling difficulty as a dysphonetically spelled word that literally cannot be read. In other words, "a spelling error is not a spelling error is not a spelling error."

Of paramount importance to us is that an error analysis system should be applicable to spelling in context, as opposed to words in given lists. In other words, errors should be clearly emergent from the student's own writing and not, in a sense, contrived by having the student respond to a pre-established list of words which are likely to be misspelled by many spellers. We have been particularly concerned that we view spelling as an element of the writing experience and not as a skill apart from writing. Accordingly, we have developed an error analysis system (see Figure 3.1) that can be applied to the everyday writing experiences of students.

Four basic characteristics of spelling are considered:

1. *Language*. Since the purpose of spelling is to convey meaning, we begin with language. Many spelling errors are language-based. Principal errors of this type include the following:

   A. Wrong or missing affixes

      Examples:

      (1) words in which the prefix has been substituted erroneously, e.g., *unproper* rather than *improper*

LANGUAGE BASE	LEARNED LEXICON	ORTHOGRAPHIC CONVENTIONS	ANOMALIES
wrong or missing affixes	homonym-type confusion	spelling-rules errors	transposed letters/syllables
invented words	compound-word errors		bizarre spellings
foreign language or dialectal interference	spelling ingenuity	faulty phoneme-grapheme correspondence	
USAGE NOTES		HANDWRITING PROBLEMS	VARIANT MISSPELLINGS

Figure 3.1. A spelling error analysis protocol by Yarborough and Silva.

    (2) words for which the inflection is missing, e.g., *test* where *tests* is indicated or *suppose* where *supposed* is indicated

B. Invented words, i.e., words that are plausible but do not exist

Examples:

    (1) *enchanged upon*, where the phrase *chanced upon* is indicated

    (2) *nodoubtly*, where *undoubtedly* is indicated

    (3) *effectant*, where *effective* is indicated

C. Foreign language or dialectal interference

(Although this category is more likely to be of significance when the instructor has the opportunity to speak with the writer personally, some forms can be assigned to fit in this category because of obvious indications within a written context.)

Examples:

(1) *vomick*, where *vomit* is indicated (southern dialect)
(2) *onde* where *wave* is indicated (French language interference)
(3) *themself*, where *themselves* is indicated (social dialect)

In addition to these types of language-based errors, there is at least one type of language-related error — i.e., usage, including problems of pronoun, preposition, and article substitution — such as the use of *I* when *me* is indicated, the use of *of* when *from* is needed, or the use of *a* when *an* is needed.

Another source of frequent errors, indirectly related to written language error, is *handwriting*, aberrant character formation that results in confusion between letters — e.g., between *m* and *n* or between *o* and *a*. Also noted here are letter reversals (*f* for *j* or *b* for *d*) and problems of erratic capitalization.

2. *Learned Lexicon*. A fortunate speller has a large number of words available that have been memorized and can be spelled virtually automatically. The development of this lexicon is highly dependent upon good visual memory of a generative type; that is, we must develop in our neurological storage facilities the memories of the visual characteristics of literally thousands of words which can be called forth automatically as we need them in writing.

The category of *learned lexicon* is used for spelling errors of the following kinds:

A. Homonym-type confusion

Examples:

(1) *to/two/too*
(2) *except/accept*
(3) *where/were*
(4) *peak/peek*

B. Compound-word errors

Examples:

(1) *alot* for *a lot*
(2) *how ever* for *however*
(3) *self contained* for *self-contained*
(4) *alright* for *all right*

C. Spelling ingenuity, i.e., principally problems of finding a grapheme to represent the schwa or sibilant, determining whether to double a consonant within the word, not writing the syncopated weak vowel, etc.

Examples:

(1) *intrest* for *interest*
(2) *desesion* for *decision*

 (3) *ambishun* for *ambition*

 (4) *incurr* for *incur*

 (5) *beligerent* for *belligerent*

3. *Orthographic Conventions.* If we do not have the precise memory of a word form available, there are several resources upon which we may rely. Spelling rules help, e.g., plural formations, dropping "silent" *e*'s before *ing*'s, etc. Also, we have a system of phoneme/grapheme correspondences with which we are familiar and which we may apply to our spelling. Errors related to faulty use of orthographic conventions include the following:

 A. Spelling-rules errors, i.e., errors that proceed from ignorance of well-known and highly productive spelling rules, such as the *i* before *e*, consonant doubling (before a suffix), and the final silent *e* rules.

 Examples:

 (1) *beleive* for *believe*

 (2) *planed* for *planned*

 (3) *it's* for *its*

 (4) *tryes* for *tries*

 (5) *wieghs* for *weighs*

 (6) *riseing* for *rising*

 (7) *gearring* for *gearing*

 (8) *heros* for *heroes*

 B. Faulty phoneme/grapheme correspondence (consisting primarily of vowel difficulties where adolescents and adults are concerned)

 Examples:

 (1) *disares* for *desires*

 (2) *moral* for *morale*

 (3) *explotation* for *exploitation*

 (4) *cloth* for *clothe*

4. *Anomalies*: When we do not have available to us a visual memory of a word and other cognitive resources fail, then spelling can go awry in very severe ways. Letters can be reversed, syllables can be transposed within letter sequences, and whole syllables can be disarranged — resulting in a wide array of bizarre spellings. In other words, there is a significant difference in the spelling needs of a person who forgets the second "r" in *arrange* or leaves the "e" off the end of *believe* and those of one who writes in an unintelligible manner that is beyond deciphering. Persons who make a number of errors of this severe type may have specific and pronounced learning disabilities affecting spelling skills or have unique spelling disorders that require intensive treatment or adaptation.

Examples of anomalous spellings are as follows:

A. Transposed letters/syllables, where we notice that sets involving vowels and liquids are probably the most common

   Examples:

   (1) *pulbic* for *public*
   (2) *feul* for *fuel*
   (3) *solgan* for *slogan*
   (4) *commerical* for *commercial*
   (5) *villian* for *villain*
   (6) *peopel* for *people*

B. Bizarre spellings, in which dysphonetic substitutions are made or whole syllables are lost or added

   Examples:

   (1) *frm* for *form*
   (2) *perhappes* for *perhaps*
   (3) *destrotion* for *destruction*
   (4) *cearrar* for *career*
   (5) *elemiation* for *elimination*

In addition to the frequent incidence of gross anomalies, another characteristic of the writing of certain disabled spellers is variant misspellings or spelling the same word several different ways within one writing experience, e.g., *producted*, *prodect*, and *producked* for *product* or *cafen* and *cafeen* for *caffeine*. Noting the occurrence of variant misspellings is important, since they may suggest extreme insecurity on the part of the speller. They may also be graphic evidence of severe visual perception/memory disabilities which prevent appropriate monitoring of the writer's written forms. Such a speller cannot validate forms as being correct or incorrect and therefore may produce a melange of forms for one word.

Our error analysis system is primarily a screening device which should clearly identify the seriously disabled speller and classify the primary types of error found in the writing of all students. It can be applied again and again, and indeed should be, as writing experiences are repeated. For those students whose spelling is distorted or distressed to the point of the preponderance of errors being of the anomaly or variant-misspelling type, a case study is recommended. For most spellers, however, including the moderately learning disabled, the application of this error-analysis system should allow the teacher to pinpoint the students' needs and thereby maximize instructional effort in spelling. The student can be helped to internalize his or her spelling needs and to become a partner in an all-out spelling improvement effort when specific instructional goals are clearly identified.

Many adolescent and adult spellers give up trying to overcome their spelling problems because of the enormity of the task of learning to spell thousands of words, one word at a time. When these troubled spellers can be shown, however, that the learning of one spelling principle can make possible the correct spelling of hundreds of words or even a small number of frequently used words, motivation can usually be maintained.

It is suggested that a form similar to the one in Figure 3.1 be completed for each major writing experience of the student and kept on file so that progress in spelling can be noted. We have observed that many students' errors move from the anomaly category to the learned lexicon category as improvement is realized.

Since this error classification system is relatively objective and easy to apply, it can be taught to student readers and/or parent readers so that teachers with large classes can be assisted in its application. Another advantage of this mechanism is its use as a tool in objectifying student progress. It offers a needed alternative to many of today's standardized measures which ask students to select a correctly spelled word from among several or a misspelled word from among several and therefore do not require the student to spell per se. The proposed system addresses spelling at its source — in the on-going writing experiences of the student.

REFERENCES

Avakian-Whitaker, H., and H. A. Whitaker. The spelling errors of children with communication disorders: a preliminary classification. *Linguistics*, 1973, *115*,105-118.

Cromer, R. F. Spontaneous spelling by language-disordered children. In U. Frith, ed., *Cognitive Processes in Spelling*. London: Academic Press, 1980.

Frith, U. Unexpected spelling problems. In U. Frith, ed., *Cognitive Processes in Spelling* . London: Academic Press, 1980.

Holmes, D. L., and R. J. Peper. An evaluation of the use of spelling error analysis in the diagnosis of reading disabilities. *Child Development*, 1977, *48*,1708-1711.

Hotopf, N. Slips of the pen. In U. Frith, ed., *Cognitive Processes in Spelling* . London: Academic Press, 1980.

Shaughnessy, M. *Errors and Expectations*. New York: Oxford University Press, 1977.

Venezky, R. L. From Webster to Rice to Roosevelt. In U. Frith, ed., *Cognitive Processes in Spelling*. London: Academic Press, 1980.

4

A Comparison of Learning Disabled and Mentally Retarded Students on the
Test of Adolescent Language

Berttram Chiang, Marilyn Fender, Mary Dale, Harold Thorpe

LANGUAGE DEFICITS have been a major concern when identifying and programming the learning disabled and mentally retarded (Schiefelbush 1970; Alley and Deshler 1979; McLoughlin and Lewis 1980). The current federal definition for learning disabilities states, "learning disabilities means those children who have a disorder . . . involved in understanding or in using language, spoken or written" (Federal Register 1977). Virtually all definitions of learning disabilities identify language as a major deficit area. With regard to the learning disabled adolescent, the Kansas Research Institute on Learning Disabilities (Warner, Alley, Schumaker, Deshler, and Clark 1980) stated that word decoding, word identification, and written production are three of the seven high probability deficit areas for the adolescent learning disabled student. Two of the other four high probability deficit areas, test taking and study skills, are also highly language oriented. Mentally retarded students also have extensive problems in usage of language (Schiefelbush 1970; Bloom 1974; Wiig and Semel 1976). A major topic of investigations funded by the federal government, particularly The National Institute of Child Health and Human Development, during the past 15 years has been the complex areas of language functions of the mentally retarded (Schiefelbush 1970).

Whereas there has been considerable discussion about the language problems of both the mentally retarded (MR) and the learning disabled (LD) students, little research has been done to measure the extent of differences in language between these two groups. Neither have the language abilities of handicapped adolescents been adequately explored (Hammill, Brown, Larsen, and Wiederholt 1980). The literature on language differences among the handicapped adolescent is indeed sparse and warrants extensive concentration of efforts by researchers concerned about the education of the handicapped.

A small amount of research data is available. La Brant (1933) analyzed written language of more than a thousand subjects, age 9 to 70 with IQ's between 65 and 150 + . Changes in use of embedded and subordinate clauses were found to be the main factor related to differences in language skills. In a longitudinal study of 388 K-12 students (Loban 1976) speaking and listening appeared to be critical dimensions of language with the highest correlations found to be between intelligence and vocabulary. Differences among written language skills as measured by the *Test of Written Language* (Hammill and Larsen 1978) were examined in two studies where learning disabled and normal students were compared (Poplin, Gray, Larsen, Banikowski, and Mehring 1980; Chiang and Fender, 1982). In general, learning disabled students in both studies were found to be approximately one standard deviation below the normal student in their Written Language Quotient.

Various isolated areas of language such as vocabulary, listening and grammar have been frequently measured in a variety of studies. Miscellaneous subtests and scales however do not look at the total profile of an adolescent's language abilities. Additionally the tests and subtests frequently used have all been standardized on different populations. This makes it very difficult to do any meaningful comparisons between tests (Salvia and Ysseldyke 1979).

The purpose of this study is to compare the profiles of the learning disabled and mentally retarded on the *Test of Adolescent Language* (TOAL) to determine whether the test does differentiate the two groups. A second purpose of the study is to investigate the relationship among multidimensional assessment of language and school achievement for LD and MR students.

METHOD

Subjects

The subjects in this study were 136 LD students (M = 94, F = 42) and 28 MR students (M = 15, F = 13) enrolled in thirteen special education classes. They were identified using the state of Wisconsin criterion. Their ages ranged from 11 years 11 months through 18 years 5 months with an LD mean age of 14.76 and an MR mean age of 15.05. These students were placed in grades 6 through 12. The MR students had a mean IQ score of 72.15 and the LD students a mean IQ of 92.86. The students were from rural communities and small towns in East Central Wisconsin.

Procedure

Thirteen teachers who volunteered for the study were given three hours of training in the administration of the TOAL. They then administered all tests during a subsequent two-month period. In addition, they were asked to tabulate for ech student the following data: chronological age, grade level, Wechsler

Intelligence Scores(WISC-R or WAIS), and *Wide Range Achievement Test* (WRAT) scores in Reading, Spelling and Arithmetic.

All tests were scored by the study's investigators. Scorer reliability was assessed on the three TOAL subtests that contain a subjective component in the scoring; Speaking/Vocabulary, Writing/Vocabulary, and Writing/Grammar. The reliability check was conducted by randomly selecting 6 of the 17 classroom results and determining the percent of agreement in the scoring of two raters. The raters did not score the tests independently. That is, all six tests were scored first by one rater and when the second rater scored the tests it was with knowledge of the scoring results of the first rater. Percent of agreement was consistently high, being either 91% or 92% for each of the three subtests.

Instrumentation

The TOAL was used to examine the language performance of the subjects of this study. The TOAL is a standardized norm referenced instrument designed to measure a combination of six dimensions of language: written form, spoken form, receptive systems, expressive systems, semantic features (vocabulary) and syntactic features (grammar). These six areas are matrixed in the test design to form eight subtests measuring all possible combinations of the six dimensions. The eight subtests yield scaled scores with a mean of ten and a standard deviation of three. Combinations of the eight subtests form ten composite scores indicated by quotients with a mean of 100 and a standard deviation of 15. These composite categories are Listening, Speaking, Reading, Writing, Spoken Language, Written Language, Vocabulary, Grammar, Receptive Language

Table 4.1

Means, Standard Deviation, and Ranges of the Learning Disabled and Mentally Retarded Students on the TOAL Subtests

Subtests	LD	(N = 136)	MR	(N = 28)
	X	Range (SD)	X	Range (SD)
Listening/Vocabulary	5.09	1-13 (3.42)	2.09	1-6 (1.51)
Listening/Grammar	3.52	1-15 (2.95)	2.19	1-12 (2.54)
Speaking/Vocabulary	6.57	1-15 (3.71)	3.95	1-7 (1.59)
Speaking/Grammar	6.35	1-17 (3.24)	5.28	1-11 (2.67)
Reading/Vocabulary	3.71	1-11 (2.42)	2.05	1-4 (1.02)
Reading/Grammar	4.84	1-13 (2.78)	2.62	1-10 (2.69)
Writing/Vocabulary	4.96	2-17 (2.83)	3.76	1-7 (1.64)
Writing/Grammar	5.63	1-13 (2.84)	3.91	2.7 (1.34)

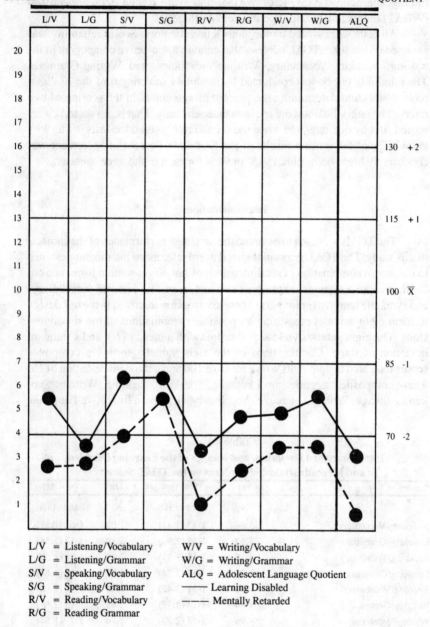

SUBTEST SCALED SCORES									COMPOSITE QUOTIENT
	L/V	L/G	S/V	S/G	R/V	R/G	W/V	W/G	ALQ

L/V = Listening/Vocabulary   W/V = Writing/Vocabulary
L/G = Listening/Grammar   W/G = Writing/Grammar
S/V = Speaking/Vocabulary   ALQ = Adolescent Language Quotient
S/G = Speaking/Grammar   ——— Learning Disabled
R/V = Reading/Vocabulary   ‑‑‑‑ Mentally Retarded
R/G = Reading Grammar

Figure 4.1. Scaled scores of learning disabled and mentally retarded students.

and Expressive Language. Additionally, an overall Adolescent Language Quotient (ALQ) with the same 100 mean and 15 standard deviation can be derived.

The Wide Range Achievement Test (Jastak and Jastak 1978) was used to measure achievement in reading, mathematics, and spelling. There is no overall score yielded from the WRAT. However standard scores are achieved in each of the three subtest areas, all having a mean of 100 and a standard deviation of 15.

The Wechsler Intelligence Scale for Children-Revised (WISC-R) (Wechsler 1974) was used as the intelligence test for the majority of the students. The WISC-R provides IQ scores; Verbal IQ, Performance IQ, and Full Scale IQ; based on a group of five subtests for verbal and five subtests for performance measures. The mean for all three IQ's is 100 with a standard deviation of 15. In a few cases the *Wechsler Adult Intelligence Scale* (WAIS) was used which is basically the same design as the WISC-R but has a higher upper age limit.

RESULTS

Means, standard deviations, and ranges of the learning disabled and mentally retarded groups are presented in Table 4.1 for each of the eight subtests. Inspection of these results reveals that all of the subtest means deviate markedly from the expected mean of 10. However, the wide range of scores, particularly for the LD group, suggests that some of the LD students are not distinguishable from normal adolescents. A profile of the subtest scaled scores for the two groups shown in Figure 4.1 depicts the slightly higher scores on the two Speaking subtests for both LD and MR groups.

Table 4.2 presents the means, standard deviations, and t-test results for the LD and the MR samples on the ALQ, the different TOAL composite scores, the IQ scores, and the WRAT scores. A comparison of the ALQ and IQ scores reveals that both LD and MR samples' ALQ scores are at least one standard deviation below their respective IQ scores. Among the various composite scores, both groups scored higher on Speaking, followed by Writing, Listening, and Reading. In terms of the two forms, Spoken Language Performance was better than that of Written Language for both groups. With regard to the two systems, both groups scored higher in Expressive Language than in Receptive Language. As for the two linguistic features included, the LD sample's scores in Vocabulary and Grammar were about the same, whereas the MR sample did somewhat better in Grammar than in Vocabulary.

A t-test analysis of the MR and LD group scores on the ALQ, the different TOAL composite scores, IQ scores, and WRAT scores indicate a significant difference (p. < .05) in favor of the LD group, on all variables. Every area of analysis except the TOAL Speaking composite score, WRAT Math, and WRAT Spelling achieved a statistical significance of .001 or less.

Table 4.2

Means, Standard Deviations, and T-Test Comparing the Learning Disabled, and The Mentally Retarded Samples on TOAL Composites, WISC-R, and WRAT Scores

| Areas of Analysis | LD (N = 136) | | MR (N = 28) | | |
	X̄	SD	X̄	SD	t
ALQ	65.93	12.75	54.70	6.17	4.54*
Listening	66.44	15.31	54.66	8.70	3.94*
Speaking	78.79	17.40	67.76	9.80	3.25†
Reading	65.97	12.32	55.09	7.82	4.49*
Writing	71.81	12.11	63.00	7.12	3.71*
Spoken Language	69.26	15.07	56.90	6.90	4.24*
Written Language	65.64	11.71	54.95	6.71	4.67*
Vocabulary	67.53	15.22	54.09	5.32	4.61*
Grammar	67.36	12.85	57.85	9.38	3.71*
Receptive Language	63.01	12.84	52.42	6.66	4.24*
Expressive Language	72.10	15.19	61.71	7.86	3.52*
IQ	92.86	9.39	72.15	10.01	10.56*
WRAT Reading	78.19	13.00	65.85	7.90	4.83*
WRAT Math	78.07	9.11	74.13	7.15	2.15‡
WRAT Spelling	76.99	9.10	75.14	8.13	.99‡

* Significant at: .001 level

† Significant at: .01 level

‡ Significant at: .05 level

In addition, the multiple regression procedure was applied for the LD and the MR samples separately to analyze the relationship between the ALQ, the WISC-R IQ and the WRAT variables. The multiple regression data are presented within Table 4.3. It can be seen that 53 percent of variance in the LD sample's ALQ is explained by the IQ score alone with the three WRAT subtest scores adding an increment of 15 percent to the variance. For the MR sample, a substantial proportion (68 percent) of variance in ALQ can be accounted for by the WRAT Reading score. The contribution of WRAT Spelling score, when used in conjunction with WRAT Reading, account for 89 percent of the total variance.

DISCUSSION

The significantly lower scores of the LD and the MR samples in comparison to those of the regular sample used in the standardization group and reported in the

Table 4.3
Multiple Regression on the ALQ for LD and MR Groups

Variable	Multiple R	R^2
LD		
IQ	.728	.53
WRAT (Math)	.809	.65
WRAT (Reading)	.823	.67
WRAT (Spelling)	.826	.68
MR		
WRAT (Reading)	.828	.69
WRAT (Spelling)	.944	.89
Age	.973	.95
IQ	.983	.97

test manual, suggest that special education students either have global language deficits or could not adjust to the emphasis on relational meaning in the format of the test. The student is required to select more than one semantically or syntactically acceptable response for each test item in Listening/Vocabulary, Listening/Grammar, Reading /Vocabulary, and Reading/Grammar. The complexity of this task may have been too difficult for the LD and MR students. Such an explanation is further supported by the finding that the MR students scored highest in the Speaking/Grammar subtest which uses the sentence imitation method, requiring the most mechanical type of responses.

The mean scores obtained in this study for the LD and MR groups were consistently lower than those presented for similar groups within the TOAL manual. It is not clear whether these differences are attributable to subject characteristics or different curricular emphases. Further research needs to be designed and conducted to determine the language performance levels of LD and MR adolescents. In addition, further studies are needed to determine how much of the difference between the LD and MR samples is due to language per se rather than academic difficulties or deficits related to cognitive factors such as attention, memory or motivation.

The multiple regression finding suggests an interrelationship among language, intelligence and achievement. Such a finding is not surprising. The indication that TOAL, WISC-R, and WRAT share common attributes is most notable with the more homogeneous MR sample.

In summary, the TOAL provides a measure which does differentiate the LD, the MR, and the normal groups. In addition, the study provides empirical evidence to support the relationship of the TOAL with two of the most commonly used measures of achievement and intelligence, WRAT and WISC-R.

REFERENCES

Alley, G., and D. Deshler. *Teaching The Learning Disabled Adolescent: Strategies and Methods*. Denver: Love, 1979.

Bloom, L. Talking, understanding and thinking. In R. L. Schiefelbush and L. L. Lloyd, eds., *Language Perspectives, Acquisitions, Retardation and Intervention*. Baltimore, Md.: University Park Press, 1974, pp.283-311.

Chiang, B., and M. Fender. "A Comparison of Performance Between Learning Disabled and Normal Adolescents on *The Test of Written Language*." Unpublished manuscript, 1982.

Federal Register. *The Education of All Handicapped Children Act of 1975, Regulations*. August 27, 1977.

Hamill, D., V. L. Brown, S. C. Larsen and J. L. Wiederholt. *Test of Adolescent Language: A Multidimensional Approach to Assessment*. Austin, Tex.: PRO-ED Publishing Co., 1980.

Hammill, D., and S. Larsen. *The Test of Written Language*. Austin, Tex.: PRO-ED, 1978.

Jastak, J. F., and S. Jastak. *Wide Range Achievement Test*. Wilmington, Del.: Jastak Assoc., 1978.

La Brant, L. L. "A Study of Certain Language Developments of Children in Grades 4 to 12 Inclusive." *Genetic Psychology Monograph, 14* (1933): 351-491.

Loban, W. *Language Development Kindergarten Through Grade Twelve*. Urbana, Il.: National Conference of Teachers of English, 1976.

McLoughlin, A., and B. Lewis. *Assessing Special Students: Strategies and Procedures*. Columbus, Oh.: Charles E. Merrill, 1981.

Poplin, S., R. Gray, S. Larsen, A. Banikowski, and T. Mehring. "A Comparison of Components of Written Expression Abilities in Learning Disabled and Non-Learning Disabled Students at Three Grade Levels." *Learning Disabilities Quarterly, 3* (1980):46-53.

Salvia, J., and J. E. Ysseldyke. *Assessment in Special and Remedial Education*. Boston: Houghton Mifflin, 1979.

Schiefelbush, R. L., ed., *Language of the Mentally Retarded*. NICHD-Mental Retardation Research Center Series. Baltimore, Md.: University Park Press, 1970. Introduction xvii to xxii.

Warner, M., G. Alley, J. Schumaker, D. Deshler, and F. Clark. *An Epidemiological Study of Learning Disabled Adolescents in Secondary Schools: Achievement and Ability, Socioeconomic Status, and School Experiences*. Lawrence, Ka.: Institute for Research on Learning Disabilities, 1980.

Wechsler, D. *Wechsler Intelligence Scale for Children-Revised*. New York: Psychological Corporation, 1974.

Wiig, E. H., and E. M. Semel. *Language Disabilities in Children and Adolescents*. Columbus, Oh.: Charles E. Merrill, 1976.

5

The Performance of Learning Disabled and Nonhandicapped Children on a Referential Communication Task

Jean Kidder

Referential communication requires that a speaker construct a message which will allow someone else (the listener) to know what the message refers to in a communicative setting (Glucksberg, Krauss, and Higgins 1975). The listener selects or identifies a target stimulus (the referent) from among a set of implicit or explicit alternatives (nonreferents). Numerous studies on referential communication skills of nonhandicapped children have been reported in the literature. However, only a few investigators have examined the performance of children with learning disabilities on such tasks (Bryan, Donahue, and Pearl 1981; Noel 1980).

The results of referential communication studies have frequently been interpreted within the framework of Piaget's concept of egocentrism. Egocentrism refers to the inability to shift one's mental perspective and consider another person's point of view. Recently, investigators have argued that egocentrism is too general a concept to be very useful and have started to examine the components of referential communication (Glucksberg, Krauss, and Higgins 1975; Asher 1978). By looking at the various parts of the task it is possible to locate where breakdowns occur. This is especially important when examining the performance of children with learning disabilities since their abilities and disabilities vary markedly from child to child.

This study compared how learning disabled and nonhandicapped children describe and receive information in a referential communication task. An extended version of the Krauss, Glucksberg, and Higgins (1975) model was used in the study to analyze the children's performance. The Krauss, Glucksberg, and Higgins model consists of four components: the speaker's sensitivity to the referent/nonreferent array, speaker's sensitivity to characteristics of the listener, the effect of feedback on the speaker's descriptions, and the role of the listener. Two additional components were added: the size and structure of the child's linguistic repertoire and the role of memory (specifically, the ability to deal with varying number and type of distinguishing features).

To determine the differences between the learning disabled and nonhandicapped children the following questions were asked: Do the number and type of distinguishing features of the stimulus pictures play a significant role? What is the effect of an extraneous picture in an array? Do children give extraneous information when describing pictures? What type of vocabulary substitutions do the children make? What type of syntactic structures do they use? Do they spontaneously ask for clarification when they are the listener? How does feedback from the adult listener affect the children's descriptions?

METHOD

Selection of Subjects

Twenty first and second graders with language related learning disabilities (aged 6;6 8;8, $\overline{X} = 7$) and twenty nonhandicapped children (aged 6;6-8;2; $\overline{X} = 7;2$) were subjects; there were five girls and fifteen boys in each group. The learning disabled children had been previously identified by special education personnel after classroom teachers had filled out informal checklists, pinpointing areas in which a child was having problems. All available test data were checked in order to fully describe the children's abilities/disabilities. The children were of average intelligence as measured by individualized verbal intelligence tests (WISC-R, WISC, PPVT); they had problems in listening comprehension, following directions, classifying, determining precise word meanings and/or or sequencing. No child had severe articulation, syntactic, or visual perceptual problems as indicated on the tests used or by teacher evaluation. The children were from monolingual (English), middle to lower middle income families as determined by a modified version of the Hollingshead scale (described in Kidder 1980). All of the learning disabled children were in a regular first or second grade classroom and attended a resource room from 25 to 60 percent of the school day.

Twenty nonhandicapped children were chosen in the following manner: the first and second grade teachers of the learning disabled children were asked to make a list of the children in their classrooms who appeared to have normal intelligence, did not exhibit learning disabilities, and who were from middle to lower middle income families in which only English was spoken. The accuracy of the teachers' perceptions of the intellectual ability of the children was checked with the children's performance on a standardized test. Since the children had not been given an IQ test, the scores of the Clymer Barrett Prereading Battery, Form B, were used. To be eligible for the nonhandicapped group a child had to score at the fourth stanine or better. The income level of the parents was checked with the modified version of the Hollingshead scale. From the children who met the above criteria twenty children were randomly selected.

The proportion of boys and girls from each classroom was equal to that in the learning disabled group.

Procedure

All children participated in three experimental sessions. The Krauss and Glucksberg paradigm (1966, 1967, 1969) was used with an adult and child seated at a table with a divider between them. The two had identical arrays of pictures in front of them. The materials consisted of three sets of pictures of farm animals drawn on strips of mat board. From two to eight pictures were drawn in 2x3 inch rectangles on the mat board strips. The stimulus pictures varied along five parameters (species, color, pattern, size, and position in space) with each parameter having two values (e.g., species — cow and pig). There were four levels of complexity of pictures — pictures with two, three, four and five distinguishing features — with four pictures at each level. A detailed description of the selection of distinguishing features for each stimulus picture and the position of the stimulus pictures in the array are given in Kidder (1980). Before the experimental sessions all children were given a pretest to see if they could identify and describe the distinguishing features of the pictures. Two pictures which varied by only one distinguishing feature were presented simultaneously. This provided an opportunity to see whether the children could use language contrastively (i.e., name just the attribute that distinguishes the target stimulus from its alternatives). Children had to identify 80 percent or more of the pictures correctly to be included in the study.

The child and adult took turns at being the speaker and listener. The speaker described a target picture to the listener who identified the picture in his array. All children played the speaker role in the first session so that the descriptions they used would not be influenced by the structures used by the adult speaker. The adult listener held up the picture that the child had described to him and asked, "Is it this one?" The child was told to acknowledge if the response was correct. If the response was not correct the adult replaced the picture and the child described the stimulus picture again. If the child's description was ambiguous the adult listener asked for clarification. The adult used implicit and explicit feedback, always using implicit feedback first. When the child gave an incomplete description the adult listener would say, "I'm not sure. Can you tell me again?" If the child speaker then did not produce an adequate message the adult listener again gave implicit feedback. If the child's message was still not adequate the listener asked for explicit clarification in the form of specific questions (e.g. "What color is it?"). About a week later the chldren played the listener role with the same adult. The adult speaker gave accurate descriptions in the form of complete sentences (e.g. "Show me the big, red cow that's spotted."). Only two adjectives were used before the noun because it was assumed that it would be too difficult for the children to process a structure with more than two adjectives before the noun. The child was told that if he was not sure which picture the adult described he should ask for more information. If the child hesitated in choosing a picture but did not verbally express that he was confused the experimenter asked for clarification for the child using the same form of clarification that the adult listener used in the first session. (For example, the experimenter said, "I'm not sure. Can you tell me again?" or "What size is it?") In a third session the children again played the speaker role. The purpose of repeating the production task was to see if there was a marked effect on the children's descriptions after they had been exposed to the correct model used by the adult.

Each session was taped and a record sheet was filled out by the experimenter during the session. The purpose of the record sheet was to record the child's nonverbal behavior and to double check that the adult listener was correctly paying attention to which distinguishing features the child named.

RESULTS

The results obtained in the comprehension and production tasks will be discussed separately since some marked differences in performance were observed. Since many analyses were performed, the .01 level of significance was chosen for all analysis of variance tests, t tests, and Chi Square tests to minimize the acceptance of an hypothesis by chance alone. The level of significance for the Newman Keuls Multiple Method of Comparison was set at .05.

Listening Comprehension Task

The results of a 2 (group) $\times$ 4 (number of distinguishing features) analysis of variance were significant for group $(F1,39) = (18.60, p < .001)$ and approached significance for the number of distinguishing features $(F(4,36) = 3.02, .037pE.01)$. The Newman Keuls Multiple Method of Comparison showed that the learning disabled children made significantly more errors than the nonhandicapped $(\overline{X}_{LD} = 0.55, \overline{X}_{NH} = 0.10)$. For both groups of children the number of pictures identified correctly decreased as the number of features to be dealt with increased. Interaction between group and number of distinguishing features was not significant $(F(3,37) = 2.18, p > .01)$.

A 2 (group) $\times$ 5 (type of distinguishing features — i.e., species, color, pattern, position, and size) analysis of variance proved not significant

$(F(4,36) = 1.21, p > .01)$. The effect of having an extraneous picture in an array was not significant $(F = (1,39) = .01, p > .01)$. The total number of descriptions in which subvocalizations occurred was significantly greater for the learning disabled group than the nonhandicapped children $(\chi^2 (1) = 21.10, p < .01)$. Although the difference between groups in the number of children asking for clarification was not significant $(\chi^2 (1) = .4, p > .01)$, the total number of times any type of clarification was requested approached significance $(t(38) = 2.11, .05 > p > .01)$. The learning disabled group requested clarification more frequently.

Production Task

The results of a 2 (group) × 4 (number of distinguishing features) × 2 (session) analysis of variance for repeated measures were significant for group $(F(1,39) = 9.71, p < .01)$, number of distinguishing features $(F(4,36) = 40.56, p < .001)$ and session $(F(1,39) = 36.90, p < .001)$. The learning disabled children made significantly more errors than the nonhandicapped children (Newman Keuls, $\overline{X}_{LD} = 1.70$, $\overline{X}_{NH} = 1.33$). Both groups of children made significantly more errors when describing stimulus pictures with four and five distinguishing features than with two or three (Newman Keuls, $\overline{X}_5 = 2.46$, $\overline{X}_4 = 1.60$, $\overline{X}_3 = 1.43$, $\overline{X}_2 = 0.60$). More errors were made in the first session than the second ($\overline{X}_1 = 1.875$, $\overline{X}_2 = 1.156$). Interactions were not significant.

The results of a 2 (group) × 5 (type of distinguishing features) × 2 (session) analysis of variance for repeated measures were significant for type $(F(4,36) = 37.31, p < .001)$ and session $(F(1,39) = 20.78, p < .001)$ and approached significance for group $(F(1,39) = 4.33, .05 > p > .01)$. The children made significantly more errors in describing the distinguishing feature "size" ($\overline{X} = 3308.99$) than any other feature and made significantly more errors in describing "species" ($\overline{X} = 1919.35$) than "position" ($\overline{X} = 1428.66$) or "pattern" ($\overline{X} = 1411.66$). More errors were made in the first session than the second ($\overline{X}_1 = 2271.36$, $\overline{X}_2 = 1755.33$). Interactions were not significant.

The results of a 2 (group) × 3 (type of extraneous information) × 2 (session) analysis of variance for repeated measures were significant for type $(F(2,38) = 8.58, p < .001)$ but not group $(F(1,39) = 1.48, p > .01)$ or session $(F(1,39) = 0.59, p > .01)$. Both groups of children gave significantly more responses in which they made extraneous mention of "species" ($\overline{X} = 4.50$) than "other extraneous distinguishing features" ($\overline{X} = 2.44$). There was not a significant difference in the conditions of having an extraneous picture in an array vs. not having an extraneous picture in the array $(F(1,39) = .05, p > .01)$.

The number of vocabulary substitutions was analyzed with a 2 (group) × 2 (session) analysis of variance. The results were significant for group $(F(1,39)$

= 14.16, p < .01) and session ($F(1,39)$ = 17.56, p < .01). Significantly more vocabulary substitutions were produced in the first session ($\overline{X}_1$ = 1.425, $\overline{X}_2$ = 0.475). The total number of vocabulary substitutions made by the learning disabled group was significantly greater ($\overline{X}_{LD}$ = 1.375, $\overline{X}_{NH}$ = .525). When the number of individual children making substitutions was examined it was found that significantly more learning disabled children made substitutions ($\chi^2(1)$ = 8.90, p < .01). This was true for the description of every type of distinguishing feature.

Generally the two groups of children used the same syntactic structures, the most common being conjunctions. However, the nonhandicapped children used more lists to describe the stimulus pictures. The learning disabled children made more syntactic errors, some of which were never made by the nonhandicapped children. The learning disabled children had difficulty with article/noun agreement. One learning disabled child strung words together in the wrong order. Although both groups made errors involving pronouns and the verb "to have," the learning disabled children made some errors with these forms that the nonhandicapped children never made. One learning disabled child confused the auxiliary "to have" with "to be." The learning disabled children substituted object pronouns for possessive pronouns, used an indefinite pronoun when a definite one was needed and failed to maintain agreement between subject and object pronouns.

DISCUSSION

Listening Comprehension Task

The learning disabled children identified fewer stimulus pictures than the nonhandicapped children but the accuracy of responding was dependent on the same factors in both groups. The information recalled was affected by the familiarity of the subject matter. Although the difference in the number of errors made on the different types of distinguishing features was not significant, the majority of errors made by both groups were on the distinguishing features "position" and "pattern." Young children have more experience dealing with types of animals, and the color and size of an object than an object's position in space or the pattern of an object. Hence, it is not surprising that children were better able to identify the distinguishing features "species," "color," and "size" than "position" and "pattern" since familiarity is known to aid recall.

The learning disabled children did not perform as well as their nonhandicapped peers even though they used strategies to help themselves. Subvocalizing is a strategy that frequently aids recall of verbally presented material. In this study the learning disabled children subvocalized significantly more times than the nonhandicapped children. The listening task appeared to be so easy for the nonhandicapped children that subvocalizing was an unnecessary strategy. (The nonhandicapped children correctly identified 97.5 percent of the total stimulus pictures presented). Subvocalizing had a mixed effect on the performance of the learning disabled children, sometimes helping children identify the stimulus picture and other times having no effect.

The learning disabled children requested clarification more frequently although almost half of such requests were made by two children. These two children had missed many distinguishing features in the production task and hence, the model of asking for clarification had been demonstrated very often for them by the adult listener. These children were aware that they needed more information and were able to use a strategy to obtain it. Although the nonhandicapped children identified more pictures correctly, the learning disabled children made greater use of strategies which helped them monitor their performance. Further research is needed to explore the developmental implications of these findings.

Production Task

The nature of the distinguishing features is a very important factor in determining how well children do in a referential communication task. Freedle (1972) hypothesized that children process alternatives in terms of the most salient features available. Saliency or lack of it appeared to play a determining role in affecting the number of times a distinguishing feature was omitted or mentioned incorrectly. The fewest number of errors were made on the distinguishing features "pattern" and "position." These attributes are less familiar to young children than "species," "color," and "size" and possibly made a greater impact on the children, resulting in the children correctly including them in their descriptions. It should be noted that these were the two attributes that gave the children the most problems in the listening task. It would seem that different processes are involved in listening and describing in the present experiment. When children were asked to recall distinguishing features that had been verbally presented, children did best with attributes that they were familiar with. However, when they were asked to describe pictures which were visually present, the children included the less familiar attributes more often than the familiar ones.

Both groups of children gave extraneous information when describing target pictures. In the pretest only two stimulus pictures were presented at a time and children were able to give contrastive responses; very few of their responses were extraneous. However, when three or more pictures were presented simultaneously, many extraneous responses were given. This result is consistent with Ford and Olson's (1975) and Whitehurst's (1976) findings. Besides naming distinguishing features that were extraneous for a given target picture, the majority of both groups of children gave extraneous responses that were not relevant to the set of pictures as a whole (e.g., "The pig plays with his Grandpa."). This is in contrast to Ford and Olson's finding (1975) that children's descriptions were always related to the dimensions on which the stimuli varied as a whole. Since Ford and Olson's pictures were geometric shapes the difference in the nature of the stimulus pictures could account for this difference. It would be much more difficult for children to elaborate and give extraneous information about geometric forms than about farm animals.

The presence of an extraneous picture did not affect the children's performance. This finding would give support to Alvy's conjecture (1968) that children do not engage in a comparison process when describing a target picture. In the present study the experimenter told the children to "look at all the pictures" then paused before finishing the instructions. Many children made a sweeping motion which superficially appeared to be an examination of the various pictures. However, it was the experimenter's impression that the children were simply paying lip service to the instructions and weren't really examining the array. The children's behavior indicated that they were not sensitive to the referent/nonreferent array.

The domain of discourse is a very important factor in determining how well children will do on a referential communication task. Obviously children can best describe the objects for which they have the appropriate vocabulary. E. Clark (1972) found that children make vocabulary substitutions between words that share features of meaning; substitutions are generally from the same semantic field. For both groups of children the most frequent vocabulary substitutions were made on the distinguishing feature "size." This is not a surprising result since "size" is a relational term. Relational terms present special problems for children as discussed by E. Clark (1971). Also, the stimulus pictures were not identical in size (i.e., "the big cow" was larger than "the big pig"). This factor could have contributed to children giving inconsistent and/or ambiguous responses.

The learning disabled children made significantly more vocabulary substitutions, some of which were qualitatively different from those made by the nonhandicapped children. The nonhandicapped children's substitutions were always from the same semantic field as the given attribute. In contrast, several learning disabled children gave substitutions for the attribute "pattern" which were from different semantic fields but were visually similar to the given attribute (e.g., "stripes" were described as "ribs" and "polka dots" were described as "periods" and "pimples"). A few learning disabled children used gestures to describe the distinguishing features "size" and "position." When asked "Where is the cow?" one child replied, "Right here" while simultaneously pointing to the picture. Learning disabled children gave the opposite value of the distinguishing feature for "position," "species," and "color" while the nonhandicapped children did not. (Both groups of children gave the opposite value for the distinguishing feature "size.") In addition, the responses of the learning disabled children tended to be more ambiguous (e.g., "a cow on the line" was described as "lines up under his feet" and "the cow's down on the floor"). The greater number of vocabulary substitutions made by the learning disabled children could either be due to their having less developed linguistic repertoires or not having access to a lexical item when it is needed. Since the children were pretested and could identify and name the distinguishing features, it appears that the problem is one of retrieval.

The most common syntactic structure used by both groups of children was conjunctions. Ford and Olson (1975) hypothesized that children use conjunctions so as not to violate adjective ordering rules. The nonhandicapped children used more lists to describe the stimulus pictures. Listing attributes (omitting the verb) is an efficient, effective way to give the listener the needed information. The nonhandicapped children's more extensive use of lists could be due to the fact that they were more confident about what information they needed to give the listener.

The effect feedback had on a speaker reformulating his message within the same trial was examined. In general the two groups of children performed similarly to the first implicit request for clarification. Feedback had a mixed effect, producing the desired result (i.e. addition, clarification, or correction of a distinguishing feature) approximately half the time. The second implicit request for clarification was more effective with the nonhandicapped children than the learning disabled children. In the first session the nonhandicapped children gave more responses in which they added, clarified, or corrected a distinguishing feature. Both implicit requests for clarification resulted in learning disabled children giving more extraneous or erroneous responses than the nonhandicapped children. Hence, it is concluded that learning disabled children had more difficulty responding to implicit requests for information. This is in keeping with Prinz's finding (1978) that language disordered children were delayed in their ability to comprehend indirect requests. Perhaps the learning disabled children do not understand exactly what is being requested or have difficulty in supplying information on demand.

Explicit feedback was also more effective with the nonhandicapped children. The nonhandicapped children were better able to respond to the direct questions that the adult listener asked (e.g., "What color is it?"). Bryan (1976) found that peers asked learning disabled children questions less frequently than nonhandicapped children. It is likely that learning disabled children have had less experience in responding to questions. Lack of ability to respond appropriately, lack of communicative experience, and lack of confidence could contribute to the difficulty that learning disabled children have in responding to the adult's questions.

CONCLUSIONS

In general, the two groups of children encoded and decoded descriptions in a similar fashion. The most significant difference was the learning disabled children's greater difficulty in effectively using their lexical repertories. The greater frequency of vocabulary substitutions given by the learning disabled children indicated a qualitative as well as quantitative difference. This difference appears to account for the learning disabled children's poorer performance in both the listening and speaking tasks in terms of accuracy.

The ability to communicate accurately and effectively is a skill that is needed throughout a person's lifetime. Unfortunately speaking and listening skills have not received much attention in the school curriculum. Recently the Office of Education has added these skills to the list of basic skills which must be taught. However, effective training of listening and speaking skills will not happen automatically. Many special education personnel ignore development of skills in language usage and instead focus on instruction in structural competence; this is in part due to the paucity of materials available. Sound curriculum materials for increasing learning disabled children's use of language are needed; before such materials can be designed it is necessary to be able to describe the similarities and differences between nonhandicapped and learning disabled children in their language usage. The present study is a preliminary attempt to try to identify some of the similarities and differences in the way learning disabled and nonhandicapped peers use language. Training children who are deficient in listening and speaking skills must be an integral part of the school curriculum.

REFERENCES

Alvy, K. "Relation of age to children's egocentric and cooperative communication." *Journal of Genetic Psychology* 112 (1968): 275-286.

Asher, S. R. "Referential communication." In G. J. Whitehurst & B. J. Zimmerman, eds., *The Functions of Language and Cognition*. New York: Academic Press, 1978.

Bryan, T., M. Donahue, & R. Pearl "Studies of learning disabled children's pragmatic competence." *Topics in Learning and Learning Disabilities 1(2)* (1981): 29-40.

Bryan, T., R. Wheeler, J. Felican & T. Henek " 'Come on, dummy:' An observational study of children's communications." *Journal of Learning Disabilities* 9 (1976): 661-669.

Clark, E. "On the acquisition of the meaning of 'before' and 'after.' " *Journal of Verbal Learning and Verbal Behavior* 10 (1971): 266-275.

Clark, E. "On the child's acquisition of antonyms in two semantic fields." *Journal of Verbal Learning and Verbal Behavior* 11 (1972): 750-758.

Ford, W., & D. Olson "The elaboration of the noun phrase in children's descriptions of objects." *Journal of Experimental Child Psychology* 19 (1975): 383-400.

Freedle, R. "Language users as fallible information processors: Implications for measuring and modelling comprehension." In *Language Comprehension and the Acquisition of Knowledge*, edited by R. O. Freedle & J. B. Carrol. New York: V. H. Winston and Sons, Inc., 1972.

Glucksberg, S., R. Krauss and R. Weisberg, "Referential communication in nursery school children: method and some preliminary findings." *Journal of Experimental Child Psychology* 3 (1966): 333-342.

Glucksberg, S. and R. Krauss "What do people say after they have learned how to talk? Studies of the development of referential communication." *Merrill-Palmer Quarterly* 13 (1967): 309-316.

Glucksberg, S., R. Krauss and E. Higgins, "The development of referential communication skills." In *Review of Child Development Research* edited by F. Horowitz. Vol. 4, Chicago: University of Chicago Press, 1975.

Kidder, J. "The Performance of Learning Disabled and Normal Children on a Referential Communication Task." Doctoral dissertation, Boston University, 1980.

Krauss, R. and S. Glucksberg "The development of communication: competence as a function of age." *Child Development* 40 (1969): 255-266.

Noel, M. "Referential communication abilities of learning disabled children." *Learning Disability Quarterly* 3 (1980): 70-75.

Prinz, P. "The Comprehension and Production of Requests in Language Disordered Children." Doctoral dissertation, Boston University, 1978.

Whitehurst, G. J. "The development of communication: Changes with age and modeling." *Child Development* 47 (1976): 473-482.

6

Comprehension Research
New Directions and Ideas
for Learning Disabilities Teachers

Linda Mixon Clary and Karen G. Sheppo

RECENT YEARS have brought an unprecedented interest in reading comprehension, particularly in the area of research. Recent LD research has been concerned with the same problems and has yielded many of the same conclusions. Much of the data have reiterated what good teachers and specialists have known for years, while other studies have indicated some changes that need to be made and some areas that need to be strengthened. A brief summary of this research effort indicates the following conclusions that are important for inservice teachers, resource persons and parents. "First, reading can no longer be viewed as solely a "bottom-up" process in which readers sequentially progress from letter and word recognition to the extraction of meaning. Rather, reading is an interaction between these proceses and "top-down" influences, i.e. the knowledge and expectations readers bring to the printed page" (Readence 1981). As Kenneth Goodman (1982) has indicated, ". . . many educators have come to view reading as performance on tests, exercises, and workbooks." Instead it is imperative to "see reading as a process of making sense of written language, a receptive process parallel to listening." (Goodman 1982). In order to convince students of this fact, our instruction must focus on real reading, not doing dittos, marking workbooks and taking tests.

The importance of the reader's background to his understanding of what he reads cannot be overstated and is often referred to as schema theory. Schemata (singular schema) are the networks of concepts or ideas to which the reader relates newly read material, often by filling in gaps that are present in his background and by formulating hypotheses to be accepted or rejected through reading. Consequently, Durkin (1981) has written ". . . comprehension is as dependent on what is in the reader's head as it is on what is printed," and readers may make widely varied interpretations of the same text, if their backgrounds and experiences are divergent. Indeed, their decoding of the text may be exactly the same, while their comprehension is quite different. This theory reinforces the idea that teachers must give added time to background development and exploration before reading, rather than skimming over that section of their lesson plans. For this purpose, techniques such as Stauffer's Directed Reading-Thinking Activity (1960) are useful. It is also important to encourage youngsters to make their own individual predictions before reading and share them with the group, so that the various possibilities of meaning are all explored. Goodman (1982) believes the readers' experiences, attitudes, concepts, and cognitive schemes are as important to understanding as the author's background was for creation. Brown (1980) and Bransford (1979) have pointed out that the metacognitive skills, including predicting and self-monitoring, are essential to effective learning. Hence it is very important for teachers to teach students how to predict. In fact, group interaction becomes extremely important when we want students to learn different interpretations of the same materials, as is especially common in today's multicultural, mobile student populations. For example, youngsters who have never gardened may not know the meanings of stakes and beds in that context and may only recognize those terms in relation to food and rest. It is, therefore, important that teachers know the possibilities of understanding that exist among their students and give them some strategies for learning to comprehend efficiently by specific methods.

One strategy for building background is the structured overview (Barron 1969; Earle 1969). Here the teacher and/or students select important concepts and vocabulary and arrange them in a graphic design for introduction and discussion before reading. This technique can be especially helpful in content areas. It allows the teacher an opportunity to find out what students already know, fill in gaps or correct misconceptions, and teach needed vocabulary while introducing essential concepts. Vocabulary, concepts and organization would be much clearer to youngsters who saw, discussed and/or listened to explanations of these materials before reading. This technique can aid learning disabled students in clarifying their purposes for reading (Stauffer 1969; Anderson 1980) and attending to the important parts of a passage (Wong 1982).

Reading comprehension is also affected by writing styles. Writing generally follows certain conventions in order to convey meaning and emphasize specific points. Research supports the conclusion that comprehension can be improved if the readers are aware of these conventions. According to Thorndyke (1977), well-formed stories are comprehended better than poorly-formed stories. Such well-formed stories generally follow story grammars.

Story grammar refers to the structure of stories and identifies their major components. There are several story grammars in the literature, but the one proposed by Stein and Glenn (1979) outlines the components as the setting and the episode, which includes the initiating event, internal response, attempt to reach the goal, consequence and reaction. According to the Stein and Glenn outline, a story might be analyzed as shown on Figure 6.1.

Current theorists believe that many youngsters read prose successfully because they have a schema for the components of stories and read to find them.

If the story does not fit this pattern, they often realize that something is missing and has limited their comprehension. In this instance, poor comprehension may be more a result of the author's poor writing rather than any flaw in the reader's comprehension.

Maier (1980) has found that when learning disabled subjects are directed or focused to listen for certain information, their comprehension and cognitive functioning improve. It seems reasonable and likely, then, that such focusing can aid in reading comprehension also. This factor is reinforced by the findings of many studies which have indicated that stories with poor or scrambled structure lead to less speed, accuracy, comprehensibility and recall by readers (Mandler and Johnson 1977; Stein and Nezworski 1978; Thorndyke 1977).

In addition to story structures, signaling devices are used by writers to emphasize content or structure. Such signaling devices may be found in titles, headings and subheadings and/or signal words that indicate organization, e.g., "in contrast to," "however," "subsequently," "finally." Meyer, Brandt, and Bluth (1980) found that poor readers comprehended better with help in determining signaling devices.

If knowing story grammars and signal words, enhances comprehension, how can we teach them to young people? Readeance (1981) suggests a simple three-step lesson plan based on providing a model, teaching for recognition and giving practice. In modeling, the teacher verbally describes how to read a sample text by pointing out the signals and talking about them. In the recognition

---

THE TIGER'S WHISKER

Setting	Once there was a woman who lived in a forest.
Initiating Event	One day she was walking up a hill and she came upon the entrance to a lonely tiger's cave.
Internal Response	She really wanted a tiger's whisker and decided to try to get one.
Attempt	She put a bowl of food in front of the opening of the cave and she sang soft music. The lonely tiger came out and listened to the music.
Consequence	The lady then pulled out one of his whiskers and ran down the hill very quickly.
Reaction	She knew her trick had worked and felt very happy.

(Stein and Glenn 1979)

Figure 6.1.   An analysis of a story.

phase, the teacher gives examples and non-examples that will help students recognize signaling devices. For example, she might point out that "additionally," "in comparison to," and "therefore" are signal words in the following sentences:

> Additionally, the strategy helps LD students read with more comprehension, in comparison to simply reading without a specific comprehension aid. Therefore, it is worth teaching.

Finally, practice, must be planned to help students transfer their knowledge to the materials they must read. The practice can be aided at first and independent later.

The story map (Beck and McKeown 1981) is a means of guiding questioning during comprehension that can be especially helpful in teaching story grammars. It helps youngsters develop a story schema. The device is defined as "a unified representation of a story based on a logical organization of these events and ideas" (p. 914). In order to create a map, the first step is to determine the starting point of the story and list the major events and the plot of the story. In the listing, it is important to include implied ideas and the linking sections that unify the plot. Finally, with the list as a resource, questions are structured to ask about the major points of the plot as it progresses through the story. Such questioning, after a period of time, helps youngsters not only to understand plots but also aids them in recognizing when their comprehension is poor because the author has omitted something important.

Attention to signal words and story grammar helps LD youngsters, as well as anyone who experiences difficulty in comprehension, evaluate their own comprehension. Anderson (1980) and Brown (1980) have suggested that this is an essential skill for efficient readers and helps them determine when it is necessary to reread or read ahead in order to improve comprehension.

Anaphoric devices can be another deterrent to comprehension. Anaphora are words which refer to preceding concepts or words. They are used as a means of avoiding repetitions by reducing what is said. If the reader recognizes that something has been left out, and can recall the referent, there is no problem but if he or she does not recognize the deletion and/or has no instruction in learning to make these recognitions, comprehension may suffer. For example:

> John and I went to the beach. *It* was terrific! We really enjoyed it. In fact, my whole family *does*.

> John and I went to the beach. *The beach* was terrific! John and I really enjoyed *the beach*. In fact, my whole family *enjoys the beach*.

Comprehension of the above necessitates recognizing anaphoric devices and their referents. Children need more and better instruction in recognizing this characteristic of texts. Anaphora may be used as nouns, pronouns, verbs or even whole sentences. They reduce repetition and unnecessary redundancy, but they also make comprehension more difficult. Therefore, successful readers must be taught to spot them and pick out the referents. The three-step plan by Readence (1981) described above might be used to teach anaphoric devices.

Another technique developed by this author (Clary) would involve listening, reading and writing and is based on Cunningham's Listening-Reading Transfer Lesson (1975). It can be used for anaphora or any other particular structure or feature of written language. The strategy seeks not only to teach about anaphora but to help readers monitor their understanding and application. Both tasks are important metacognitive skills for the LD youngster.

First, the teacher should choose a short, interesting passage appropriate for her students that contains five or less anaphora. She then reads it to the students while displaying a printed copy on the board or a transparency or a handout with the anaphora marked. She should point out the first two anaphora and their referents very clearly and ask for volunteers to read the next one and determine its referent. This practice would continue until all were correctly chosen.

As a second step, another passage with marked anaphora would be read aloud and displayed for the group to work through. This time there should be no teacher involvement except to reiterate the goal of the reading and helping to redirect the reader as necessary.

Third, an unmarked passage with a slightly higher number of anaphoric devices should be displayed only. Again, the group would work through it.

Fourth, each individual should work through a passage independently and list the anaphora and their referents. The teacher should evaluate for mastery immediately to determine those who need this step (or previous steps) repeated.

The fifth step is aimed toward transfer and application. The teacher directs the students to their textbooks (basal readers, tradebooks or content area texts) and briefly introduces a passage with a limited number of anaphoric devices present. The students should repeat step four, and again list the anaphora and their devices for immediate evaluation. If successful, they then proceed to the final step which is independent practice on several passages suggested by the teacher and finally, completely independent reading. Given this structured instruction and practice that is multisensory in nature, learning disabled readers should find anaphoric devices much easier to comprehend. Table 6.1 summarizes the procedure.

Comprehension alone, however, is not the only important task for LD youngsters especially at the middle school, secondary and college levels. These

Table 6.1
Guided Listening-Reading-Writing Technique

1. Teacher guided reading with visual input
2. Group guided reading with visual output
3. Group unguided reading with visual input
4. Individual unguided reading on a separate *passage* with immediate evaluation
5. Individual unguided reading in *textbooks* with immediate evaluation
6. Independent practice in *textbooks*

students must be able to employ metacognitive skills as they read and study, and their mastery of these skills must lead to independence in reading and learning.

One of the metacognitive skills that efficient readers use in comprehension is clarifying the purposes for reading, generally through self-questioning and self-checking (Anderson 1980). While little empirical research has been done with learning disabled children in this area of metacognition, it has been suggested (Wong 1982) that LD children may be affected in their reading comprehension and study because they lack these self-monitoring behaviors. The behavioral observations of many teachers would tend to support the idea that LD students neither set purposes for reading nor check their understanding of the material in relation to the set purposes.

There are several reading/study techniques that may be used with the learning disabled. The SQ3R method (Robinson, 1946) uses a questioning step followed by reading to answer the questions posed. Specific modifications of this method have also been suggested. For science, the PQRST was developed by Spache and Berg (1966) and, for mathematics, the SQRQCQ by Fay (1965). While these methods are structured as far as the thinking sequence suggested, they do not require an observable response. The teacher has no concrete way to insure that each step of the procedure has been followed by the student. Another method, OK5R (Pauk 1974), does include a recording step for summarizing the main idea but does not allow for the teacher to observe the student's setting of purposes or his self-checking after reading.

The C & S Reading Technique for Independent Study (Clary and Sheppo) was developed to provide a highly organized approach to comprehending and studying content material utilizing (1) a setting of purposes for reading through self-generated questions and (2) self-checking on meeting these purposes while (3) providing for an observable response.

To begin using the C & S, the student enters the class, date, and reading assignment at the top right-hand corner of the page. He or she then divides the assignment into manageable sections using sub-chapter headings or other divisional notations. It is recommended that one sheet be used for a section of no more than four to six pages. This will depend, of course, on the ability level of the student and the concept-load of the material. The steps are then followed in alphabetical order.

A. The student writes in the overall purpose for reading that section based on the instructor's verbal directions and/or the introduction and summary paragraphs.

B. "What do you want to remember after you read?" The student looks at the bold-face type, paragraph headings, pictures, graphs, etc. and develops questions based on these. The questions are recorded.

C. The student reads and records the answer directly beside each question, correcting any questions as needed. The page number of the answer is also entered.

D. Space is provided for adding any important ideas that were not included in the original questions. Again page numbers are noted.

E. The student maintains a running list of important vocabulary words and the page on which they are found.

F. The student lists any questions that he may wish to check on with the instructor. These may be additional questions or ones listed by number.

With the initial teaching of this method, sheets with full directions should be used. As the student understands the directions he can move to sheets with only the bare directions given thus allowing for more work space.

The C & S method provides several advantages to both the student and the teacher. First, it provides the student with a structured, visually presented pattern of reading and studying. If interrupted before completing the reading section, he can easily find his place to begin again. Second, it provides the student with consolidated and organized material from which to study for examinations. For example, by covering section C, the student can attempt to recall the answers to questions posed in B. The page number provides a quick reference to locating the answer if review is needed. Third, it provides the student with concrete practice in developing the metacognitive skill of self-monitoring by practicing setting purposes for reading and checking the understanding of the material in relation to the set purposes.

For the teacher, the C & S is a concrete method for teaching and for carefully assessing the child's development of this skill. Second, it utilizes the student's own regular class assignments and allows the teacher to assess his progress on these assignments. Third, it provides organized study material for the teacher, parent, tutor, or study partner to use with the student. Finally, it fosters the eventual independence of the student by teaching him how to better comprehend and study.

For the more severely disabled reader, the work of LaBerge and Samuels (1974) appears to have important implications for the teacher of the learning disabled. Their theory of automaticity suggests that fluent readers are able to process information below the semantic level effectively (i.e. automatically) and, therefore, full attention can be given to understanding the message intended in the material. For many LD children and youth who read slowly, who repeatedly skip over unfamiliar words, and who laboriously decode phonetically, the understanding of the content is lost. Over time the student never learns to comprehend because, in fact, he has never had the practice. Full effort and attention has been directed to "saying" words which does not mean "reading". Several methods appear appropriate for getting the child to the semantic or comprehension level by increasing both his rate and fluency.

The neurological impress method (Heckelman 1969) involves the teacher and student reading aloud together. The teacher slides her finger along the line of words while she reads into the ear of the student at close range. By being exposed to (or impressed with) a correct model, rate and fluency are increased as is comprehension. Samuels' (1979) method of repeated readings also appears to increase rate, fluency and comprehension as students are directed to reread passages until a satisfactory fluency criterion is reached.

Bos (1982) has suggested that combining neurological impress with repeated readings and including a modified cloze procedure can effectively increase comprehension in children with severe reading disabilities. Perez (1981), in describing modifications of the strict cloze procedure, suggested using reading passages from content books and omitting only nouns and verbs. The difficulty of the cloze exercise can be varied by using a multiple-choice format, by requiring the student to supply the words, or by omitting a higher percentage of the words.

Given the efficiency of the aforementioned methods for improving reading comprehension, it would seem appropriate to utilize the strengths of several of these techniques and organize them into a highly structured procedure that could be used with severely disabled readers who are still faced with the demands of content reading. The ReComp method (Sheppo) aims at increasing both reading fluency and comprehension.

In addition to the several methods already noted, ReComp includes a technique, ReQuest (Manzo 1979), that aids the student in setting purposes for reading by improving his questioning behavior. ReQuest involves reciprocal questioning between student and teacher concerning the material read. Originally, questions were based on single sentences with questioning continuing until the student could predict what would happen in the remainder of the passage. In ReComp, the total passage is used as the basis of questions.

ReComp

1. Guided Listening & Visualizing
2. Neurological Impress
3. Paraphrasing/ReQuest

  4. Repeated Reading with Purpose
  5. Modified Cloze
  6. Diagram

1. *Guided Listening & Visualizing:* Through guided listening the teacher sets the purposes for listening depending on needs of the student (i.e., strengthening understanding of cause — effect) or the content of the material (i.e., steps in cell division). The student is directed to try to visualize the specific information he is to listen for.
2. *Neurological Impress:* Using the neurological impress method the teacher and student read the section.
3. *Paraphrasing/ReQuest:* The student paraphrases as much as he can remember about the passage and the specifics he was directed to listen for. The

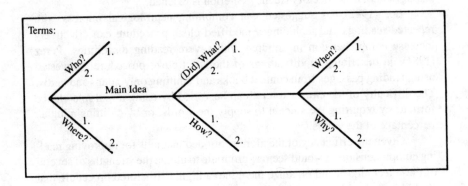

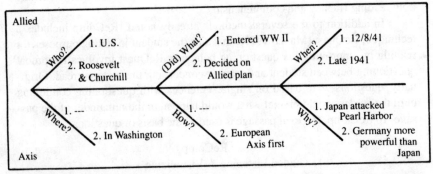

Figure 6.2. Herringbone technique, from Tierney, Readence, and Dishner (1980), pp. 83-85.

student and teacher then engage in reciprocal questioning and answering about the passage, with the teacher relating the information to the student's background.

4. *Repeated Reading with Purpose:* Specific purposes, in the form of questions, for a repeated reading are set by the student based on what he did not understand or remember. The student reads the passage again, with assistance, by the teacher, and answers the questions.

5. *Modified Cloze:* A modified cloze exercise is completed by the student. Depending on the ability of the student either a multiple-choice format or one requiring total recall is used.

6. *Diagram:* The student diagrams the important information from the passage.

In the last step "diagram" is used as a general term for requiring the student to produce a written response in an organized manner. This is seen as important in the comprehension of content material. The regular classroom generally requires the student to demonstrate his knowledge in written form. Therefore, this step will provide some practice. Also, the use of a diagram better organizes material for later study. The structured overview techniques previously noted could be used in this step as a review procedure. The Herringbone technique (Tierney, Readence, Dishner, 1980), illustrated in Figure 6.2, would also be appropriate for this step.

In conclusion, appropriate methods for improving reading comprehension have been presented. These authors urge that selected techniques be used with disabled readers to provide a structured approach to teaching comprehension. All of the methods have one extremely important feature — the student reads, reads, reads. Comprehension is developed not in isolation but in relation to the student's own content classes and background. Success is, therefore, fostered both in the regular class setting and in improved comprehension.

REFERENCES

Anderson, T. H. Study strategies and adjunct aids. In R. J. Spiro, B. C. Bruce and W. F. Brewer (Eds.), *Theoretical issues in reading comprehension: Perspectives from cognitive psychology, artificial intelligence, linguistics, and education.* Hillsdale, N.J.: Erlbaum Associates, 1980.

Barron, R. F. The use of vocabulary as an advance organizer. In H. L. Herber and P. L. Sanders (Eds.) *Research in reading in the content areas: First year report.* Syracuse, N.Y.: Reading and Language Arts Center, Syracuse University, 1969.

Beck, I.L., and M.G. McKeown. Developing questions that promote comprehension: The story map. *Language Arts*, 1981, *58*, 913-918.

Bos, C. S. Getting past decoding: Assisted and repeated readings as remedial methods for learning disabled students. *Topics in Learning and Learning Disabilities,* 1982, *1* (4), 51-57.

Bransford, J. D. *Human cognition: Learning understanding and remembering.* Belmont, Calif.: Wadsworth, 1979.

Brown, A. L. Metacognitive development and reading. In R. J. Spiro, B. Bruce, and W. F. Brewer (Eds.), *Theoretical issues in reading comprehension.* Hillsdale, N.J.: Erlbaum Associates, 1980.

Cunningham, Patricia M. The listening-reading transfer lesson. *The Reading Teacher,* 1975, *29,* 169-172.

Durkin, Delores. What is the value of the new interest in reading comprehension? *Language Arts,* 1981, *58,* 23-42.

Earle, Richard. The use of the structured overview in mathematics classes. In H. L. Herber and D. L. Sanders (Eds.), *Research in reading in the content areas: First year report.* Syracuse, N.Y.: Reading and Language Arts Center, Syracuse University, 1969.

Fay, L. Reading study skills: Math and science. In J. A. Figural (Ed.), *Reading and Inquiry.* Newark, Del.: International Reading Association, 1965.

Goodman, Kenneth. Revaluing readers and reading. *Topics in Learning and Learning Disabilities,* 1982, *1* (4), 87-93.

Heckelman, R. G. A neurological-impress method of remedial-reading instruction. *Academic Therapy,* 1969, *4,* 277-282.

LeBerge, D., and S.J. Samuels. Toward a theory of automatic information processing in reading. *Cognitive Psychology,* 1974, *6,* 293-323.

Maier, A. S. The effect of focusing on the cognitive processes of learning disabled children. *Journal of Learning Disabilities,* 1980, *13* (3), 34-38.

Mandler, Jean M. and Nancy S. Johnson. Remembrance of things passed: Story structure and recall. *Cognitive Psychology,* 1977, *9* (1), 111-151.

Manzo, A. V. The ReQuest procedure. *Journal of Reading,* 1969, *13,* (2), 123-126.

Meyer, B. D. Brandt, and G. Bluth. Use of top-level structure in test: Key for reading comprehension of ninth grade students. *Reading Research Quarterly,* 1980, *16,* 72-103.

Perez, S. A. Effective approaches for improving the reading comprehension of problem readers. *Reading Horizons,* 1981, *22* (1), 59-65.

Pauk, W. *How to study in college,* 2nd ed. Boston: Houghton Mifflin, 1974.

Readence, John. Research into practice: The center for the study of reading. *Georgia Journal of Reading,* 1980, *6* (1), 29-31.

Readence, John and John Mateja. Research into practice: Enhancing comprehension through text structure. *Georgia Journal of Reading,* 1981, *7* (1), 39-41.

Robinson, F. P. *Effective study.* New York: Harper and Bros., 1946.

Samuels, S. J. The method of repeated readings. *The Reading Teacher,* 1979. *32*, 403-408.

Spache, G. D., and P. C. Berg. *The art of efficient reading.* New York: Macmillan, 1966.

Stauffer, R. G. *Directing reading maturity as a cognitive process.* New York: Harper and Row, 1969.

———. Productive reading-thinking at the first grade level. *Reading Teacher,* 1960, *13*, 183-187.

Stein, N. L. and C. G. Glenn. An analysis of story comprehension in elementary children. R.Hillsdale (Ed.), In *New Directions in Discourse Processing* (Vol. 2). Hillsdale, N. J.: Erlbaum Associates, 1979.

Stein, N. L. and T. Nezworski. The effects of organization and instructional set story memory. (Technical Report No.29). Urbana, Illinois: University of Illinois, Center for the Study of Reading, 1978.

Thorndyke, P. W. Cognitive structures in comprehension and memory of narrative discourse. *Cognitive Psychology,* 1977, *9*(1), 77-110.

Tierney, J., J. E. Readence and E. K. Dishner. *Reading Strategies and practices: A guide for improving instruction.* Boston: Allyn & Bacon, 1980.

Wong, Bernice Y. L. Understanding learning disabled students' reading problems: Contributions from cognitive psychology. *Topics in Learning and Learning Disabilities,* 1982, *1* (4), 43-50.

7

The Child Communication Center
A Preventative Mental Health Program
for Preschool Children

Karla Hull, Sr. Kathleen McCann, Len Kruszecki

THE CHILD COMMUNICATION CENTER is a preventative mental health program for learning disabled preschoolers and their families. The purpose of our program was to provide the context of his or her interactive environment by extending our intervention process beyond academics to include facilitation of the personality development of the child, as well as to provide increased knowledge and support for parents in the art and skills of parenting, family interaction, and development, with particular emphasis on the single-parent family.

Many specialists believe that the poor self-concept and poor interpersonal relationships often seen in learning disabled children developed as a result of academic failure. This appears to be a simplification of a very complex process of development beginning at birth. In the development of the Child Communication Center program, our underlying assumptions were that the poor self-concept and difficulty in interpersonal relationships seen in learning disabled children were the result of many years of frustrating, ineffective communication attempts and delayed personality development beginning with the first interactions between parent and child. It is our contention than an effective, early identification program for learning disabled children must focus not only on remediation/compensation of academic difficulties but also upon the relationship between parent and child and personality development including the growth of a positive self concept.

Karen Horney's (1950) personality-development theories reveal that the drives to achieve competence and gain approval are crucial in the development of a stable, healthy personality. Bessell (1972) describes a preventative mental health program based on Horney's theories of personality development. This program involves three areas of experience which facilitate the development of a healthy personality. The three areas are awareness, mastery, and social interaction.

The learning disabled child is impeded in all three of the areas described by Bessell (1972) as important in the process of developing a healthy, stable personality. Learning disabled children have early perceptual, motor, and language deficits (Wiig and Semel 1980). According to Denkla (1975), 43-62 percent of all learning disabled children present a language disorder as the primary characteristic of their learning disability. Reduced facility at communication, auditory, and visual perceptual deficits and motor deficits distort the learning disabled child's awareness of what he is really experiencing, feeling, and thinking.

Mastery, as described by Bessell (1972), involves knowing one's strengths and abilities and using them effectively. Since the learning disabled child is often delayed in the acquisition of certain abilities there is an early history of failure and/or feelings of incompetence and reduced self worth. Gerber and Bryen (1981) suggest that the parents of language/learning disabled children frequently misunderstand or fail to recognize their child's problems so that by the time the child enters kindergarten he already has a subtle history of failure often unknown to the parents.

Research has consistently shown that the quality of interaction between learning disabled preschool aged children and their parents and peers is often subtly impaired. Bryan (1977) suggests that reduced comprehension of non-verbal communication may be one aspect of interpersonal relationships which affects both the attitudes of others toward learning disabled children as well as differentiates the learning disabled child from the normal child. Caracciolo and Cook (1979) indicate that communication between parents and their learning disabled children is complicated by problems of behavior, affect, language, and motivation often resulting in a frustrating breakdown of the interactive process. Thus the interpersonal relationships of the learning disabled child are often disturbed early in life and can result in secondary emotional problems.

Children do not develop in a vacuum. Their early life is intricately tied to the environment which surrounds them. With the preponderance of single parent families and the necessity of placing young children in day care facilities due to working parents, it is not surprising that there is a need for parent education and support in the art and skills of parenting and family interaction. When the family interaction is complicated by the introduction of a learning disabled child who is in need of specialized developmental support, then it is crucial that a special education preschool include parents and teachers as integral and active participants in a team designed to facilitate maximum development of the child's potential. Koppitz (1975) specifies the need for a supportive and accepting home environment and indicates that a child with normal mental potential can learn to compensate for learning disabilities if he is given sufficient time to develop and mature at this own rate without undue pressure from parents and teachers.

PROGRAM

The Child Communication Center is one program offered by the Early Child-hood Education Center, thus it exists within the context of a complete, special educational setting emphasizing cognitive, sensory-motor, language, percep-tual and social/emotional development. The Child Communication Center pro-gram is an outgrowth of research which suggests that: (a) Learning disabled children frequently experience reduced quality of interaction with peers and parents. (b) Parental involvement and support are essential to successful devel-opment and maturation of children. (c) Parents of handicapped children may need increased support and development in the areas of family interaction and parenting skills. (d) Learning disabled children are at risk for developing men-tal health problems. The Child Communication Center program is composed of four components: (1) Communication Diaries; (2) Magic Circle program; (3) Systematic Training for Effective Parenting (STEP) program; and (4) Parent Education meetings. These four areas provide parallel experiences for parent, child, and teacher and combine effectively to produce a comprehensive pre-ventative mental health program for pre-school learning disabled children and their families.

Communication Diaries

The communication diaries were developed to provide increased infor-mation sharing between parents and teachers, to provide an informal record of each child's development throughout the year, and to give parents additional learning tools to help stimulate their child's development. The diary is sent home once a month. It includes sections for teacher's comments, parent's com-ments, and activities for parents to do at home with their child. The games and activities that are included in the diary are selected from Karnes, (1977) "Learning Language at Home" program. The activities involve games in which the children are to act out directions given by the parents, recognizing what facial expressions mean, sorting clothes according to where they are worn, and other activities that concentrate on listening, speaking and manipu-lating objects in the child's environment. The diary includes instructions for doing the various activities as well as a space for parents to comment on how the child liked the game and whether or not the child was able to effectively partici-pate in the activity.

Each time the diary is sent home, one of the teachers or specialists writes a note to the parents discussing the child's growth in selected areas, any con-cerns the specialist might want to share with the parents, as well as answering any questions that parents might have asked in response to the previous month's diary. Examples of teacher's entries in the chldren's diaries are as follows:

> He has improved in many ways. When given the opportunity to lead a group, he is very effective. I hope your (parents') efforts at helping him to become more independent are going well! I have noticed that he is beginning to use his language to mediate conflicts with the other children rather than using physical force to make his needs known. This is exciting progress!

> I think she is just as delighted as we are with her progress. She's beginning to control her stuttering, rather than have it control her. The atmosphere that you are creating at home is so important in helping her feel successful. I was pleased to hear that you've been trying to reduce the competition (between sisters) for "speaking time" at home. I'm convinced that has made things much easier for her.

The parents also have a section of the diary where they can respond to the teacher's comments, express their own concerns, ask questions, or relate instances in which they have noticed their child achieving or generalizing information presented at school. Some selections from parent entries in the diary are:

> I have been aware that she has been overly hyperactive lately. I have been very concerned about this and her extra sensitivity. I don't give her very much sugar, but since I'm working and someone else is keeping her, it's hard to keep track of her daily diet. I am wondering if I should seek additional help. I would appreciate any thoughts on this.

> He continues to improve and expand his vocabulary. I'm letting him do a lot of things by himself, even helping me in the kitchen. I do have a question. How do you teach a child to think before he acts? I try to talk to him about it. However, I'm not sure I'm doing the right thing.

> Since the time we met, we have tried to give him more time in the morning so as not to rush him. This has helped a lot. Children sure do like to keep their parents "in the dark" so to speak!

Magic Circle

Magic Circle is published by Human Development Training Institute and is a daily discussion program for children which focuses on awareness of feelings, self mastery, and social interaction. This particular program was included in the Child Communication Center program because of its content and reliance on modeling techniques which Bandura (1977) describes as being one of the most effective methods of changing social behaviors. Hetherington (1965) states that greater observational learning occurs from same-sex models. Rosekrans (1967) supports the notion that people tend to match the behaviors of another person more readily when the model is more similar than dissimilar to themselves. Given the information on the increased effectiveness of modeling using same-sex models, the daily discussion groups in the Child Communication Center program are co-facilitated by an adult male and female. The co-facilitators guide the discussion insuring that all children have the opportunity to participate. The *Magic Circle* program incorporates Bangs's (1981) suggestion to introduce preschool age children to a vocabulary of affective words and to train them in the effective use of linguistic skills including the use of alternate forms of language and style to impress different listeners.

The topics of discussion in the *Magic Circle* are focused in the areas of awareness, mastery, and social interaction. The discussions in the awareness section are designed to promote "aware" communication among children who are deliberately exposed to ways in which people are alike and ways in which people differ. The children discuss and learn vocabulary that describes unpleasant feelings, negative thoughts and destructive behavior as well as pleasant thoughts and feelings, and positive behavior.

The mastery section of the *Magic Circle* is designed to promote self-confidence. The children are provided with a wide variety of tasks including linguistic, counting, dressing, health, motor and social. The tasks are presented at levels which will insure some degree of success for each child. The discussion then centers on learning what one does well and reinforcing the child's concept that he is a capable human being.

In the social interaction section, the children discuss sharing and respecting the rights of others and they learn to offer kind behavior and to ask for kind behavior. Additionally they discuss how other people's behavior affects them and how their behavior affects other people. The children learn to express themselves verbally as well as non-verbally and they learn to understand and interpret verbal and non-verbal expression in others.

Systematic Training for Effective Parenting program was developed by Dinkmeyer and McKay (1976) to expose parents to a realistic approach to rearing of children in modern society. This program teaches principles of parent-child relationships that promote responsibility, self reliance, mutual respect, and self esteem. It is designed to help parents recognize the typical but ineffective ways they and their children respond to each other and to present alternatives that can lead to more satisfying relationships. The program consists of 10 weekly meetings which include the following topics: understanding children's behavior and misbehavior, understanding more about your child and about yourself as a parent, encouragement, communication (listening to your child and expressing your ideas and feelings to your children), applying natural and logical consequences and developing parental confidence in their effective parenting skills. The STEP program for parents is particularly suitable because it parallels the topics and philosophy of the "Magic Circle" program that is used with the children at the center. Thus parents and children are both learning how to relate to one another and how to develop confidence in their own abilities. They both address the topics of how their behavior affects others. The parents as well as the children discuss respecting each others' rights.

Parent education meetings are held monthly and differed from the STEP program which emphasizes parenting skills, by providing parents with knowledge specific to the growth and development of their children. Topics were chosen for the meetings by the parents and appropriate speakers were invited to address the issues relative to the topic. Some of the topics addressed were: aggression in children, stimulating language development in children, ego development, children's sexuality, nutrition, behavior and learning, the young child and the concept of death, left handedness vs. right handedness, relationship between play and development. These monthly meetings were the only mandatory component of the Child Communication Center. The meetings were held at night, and babysitting was provided at the Center so that both parents could attend.

EVALUATION

The evaluation of the Child Communication Center program included two components. First, parents and staff completed questionnaires pertaining to the four program components. Second, the percentage of those parents attending or responding to the non-mandatory programs was computed.

Communication Diary

The evaluation of the Communication Diary by parents was overwhelmingly supportive of this program. The parents' remarks regarding the usefulness of the diary fell into three categories: (a) they learned more about their child, (b) they learned ways to interact more effectively with their child, (c) they were encouraged by the progress both they and their children were

making as reflected in comments in the diary. When asked whether the games/
activities section was difficult, 23 percent of the parents found the exercises
difficult. Reasons stated for the difficulty revolved around a central theme: that
it was difficult to find time to do the exercises with their children. Interestingly,
when asked whether the diary took up too much of their time, only 9 percent
responded yes, compared to the 23 percent who found it difficult to complete
the exercises due to "lack of time." This discrepancy may be explained by
noting additional parent comments which suggest that the parents found themselves procrastinating doing the exercises.

Most of the parents, 82 percent, felt that sending the diaries home once a
month was sufficient. The other 18 percent suggested sending the diary home
more often. The diary was not mandatory. It was sent home each month, for
nine months, with comments from specialists regardless of parental responsiveness. Only 9 percent of the parents were inconsistent in their responsiveness,
with the other 91 percent of the parents responding every month by writing
comments and doing the activities.

The specialists were supportive of the diary and felt that it provided them
with a critical, personal link to the parents. Additionally, they viewed the
diaries as preventive in that they were able to divert and direct parental behavior
more readily since they were more aware of parents' concerns and reactions to
their children. The diaries were time consuming but the specialists felt the
advantages outweighed the disadvantage of an additional time commitment.
Two drawbacks of the diaries were listed by the specialists: (a)the diary is
inappropriate for illiterate parents who are occasionally seen in this inner-city
population; (b) some parents need additional support in the form of frequent
meetings, to teach them more directly how to interact with their children.

Systematic Training for Effective Parenting (STEP)

The STEP program was consistently attended by one third of the
parents.After completing the ten weekly meetings, evaluation forms were
given to all parents who had attended the sessions. They described the main
benefits they received. Two representative statements from parents follow:

> I realized I was not alone. That we can make mistakes, parenting is not always a
> natural job. Society changes and demands create much pressure, and we cannot
> always follow steps our parents took.

> I feel it has helped me look at my children as individuals, with their own destiny,
> not just extensions of me.

Over half of the parents found the STEP program was *very* good in helping them to better understand their children's behavior and misbehavior. The other 40 percent felt the program was somewhat helpful.

Magic Circle

An evaluation was sent to parents to determine if the Magic Circle sessions had a "carry-over" effect or impact on the child's daily life at home. Excerpts from their comments follow:

The Magic Circle program has been a marvelous experience for him. He's much more communicative and sensitive to others. All of this has led to a lot less frustration in dealing with him.

He's always asking my opinion about how I feel and he seems to have more self-assurance about his self and what he's able to do.

The Magic Circle group facilitator was extremely impressed with the growth in the areas of social interaction, communication and in the development of the children's self-esteem. She also felt that the daily discussions had been instrumental in identifying problems, fears or frustrations that the children were experiencing.

Parent Education Meetings

The monthly parent education meetings were mandatory. Thus participation was generally around 95-99 percent of the parents. When asked to evaluate these meetings, parents commented that: (a)they liked the variety of topics, (b) they liked having a variety of speakers, (c) they felt the one-hour format was adequate, (d) they appreciated the child care service. Many of the parents suggested that they be allowed to bring other family members, such as aunts and grandmothers to the meetings.

An evaluation by the staff at the Center indicates that there is a definite difference in topics chosen from the first year of this program to the second. The noted difference suggests that parents are indeed being educated and are choosing topics much more specific to the learning disabilities of their children. Initially, the topics chosen were general, such as stimulating language development and the effects of drug and alcohol abuse of children. During the second year parents were asking for specific information on left vs. right handedness, how nutrition affects learning, hyperactivity and aggressiveness in children, and the development of the child's ego.

CONCLUSION

The Child Communication Center program was a successful attempt to provide knowledge and support for parents in the art and skills of parenting and family interaction as well as providing an ongoing preventative, mental health service for preschool, learning disabled children, enabling them to cope with the frustrations arising from their learning and communication disabilities. The STEP and *Magic Circle* program components provided parents and children with parallel programs designed to enhance self esteem, mastery, and social interaction. The Communication Diaries facilitated communication between parent and specialists, served as a preventative measure by allowing professionals to direct and divert parental reactions to their children's behavior, provided parents with knowledge in the areas of stimulating their child's development and increased parents' understanding of their child's achievements and deficits. The Parent Education meetings increased parental knowledge in a variety of areas relative to their child's growth and development.

Research and experience dictate that we provide early intervention aimed at the social/emotional growth of the learning disabled child as well as their different learning styles, and that this intervention process include the child's complete, interactive family, including parents, teachers, and caretakers. The Child Communication Center is one program which does provide a preventative mental health service to learning disabled preschoolers and their families.

REFERENCES

Bandura, A. *Social Learning Theory.* Englewood Cliffs, N. J.: Prentice-Hall, 1977.

Bangs, T. *Language and Learning Disorders of the Preacademic Child.* Englewood Cliffs, N. J.: Prentice-Hall, 1982.

Bessell, H. *Methods in Human Development: Theory Manual.* La Mesa, Calif.: Human Development Training Institute, 1972.

Bryan, T. H. "Learning Disabled Children's Comprehension of Non-verbal Communication." *Journal of Learning Disabilities* 10 (8) (1977).

Caracciolo, B. L., and S. Cook. "Interaction Analysis and Videotaped Self-confrontation Applied to Parent Training." *Selected Papers: Current Trends in the Treatment of Language Disorders.* American Speech-Language-Hearing Association Annual Convention, 1979.

Denkla, M. B. "Retrospective Study of Dyslexic Children (1975)." Reported in *Dyslexia: An Appraisal of Current Knowledge,* edited by A. L. Benton and D. Pearl. New York: Oxford University Press, 1978.

Dinkmeyer and McKay. *Systematic Training for Effective Parenting Program.* Circle Pines, Minn.: American Guidance Service, 1976.

Gerber, A., and D. Bryen. *Language and Learning Disabilities.* Baltimore, Md.: University Park Press, 1981.

Horney, K. *Neurosis and Human Growth.* New York: W. W. Norton, 1950.

Hetherington, E. M. "A Developmental Study of the Effects of Sex of the Dominant Parent on Sex Role Preference, Identification, and Imitation in Children." *Journal of Personality and Social Psychology* 2 (1965): 188-194.

Karnes, M. B. *Learning Language at Home Program.* 1920 Association Drive, Reston, Va.: Council for Exceptional Children, 1977.

Koppitz, E. M. *Children with Learning Disabilities: A Five-Year Follow-Up Study.* New York: Grune & Stratton, 1971.

Rosekrans, M. A. "Imitation in Children as a Function of Perceived Similarity to a Social Model and Vicarious Reinforcement." *Journal of Personality and Social Psychology* 7 (1967): 307-315.

Wiig, E. H., and E. M. Semel. *Language Assessment and Intervention for the Learning Disabled.* Columbus, O.: Charles Merrill, 1980.

ADMINISTRATION AND
POST-SCHOOL YEARS

Diagnostic Teaching Cycle
Applying a Generic Model of Instruction to Learning Disabled Students

Brenda H. Manning, Fredricka K. Reisman, Ann Neely

DIAGNOSTIC TEACHING involves selection of appropriate curriculum and teaching strategies for learners. The focus of the paper is an application of a Diagnostic Teaching Cycle (Reisman, 1982) to teaching elementary school mathematics to learning disabled students. An explanation of the processes in the Diagnostic Teaching Cycle (DTC) and an analysis of the cycle's application to classroom learning will be presented. Teachers used five thinking processes in the DTC. These processes are identifying, hypothesizing, planning, instructing, and evaluating.

PROCESS OF IDENTIFICATION

The first process, *identification*, involves the ability to investigate students' strengths and weaknesses. These may be reflected by reviewing behavior products such as achievement test scores (both standardized and teacher-made), teacher observation, and interviews. Cognitive generic factors are useful for organizing students' strengths and weaknesses during the identification process.

The term "cognitive generic factors" is used to identify those characteristics which influence learning and the rate at which knowledge is acquired. These factors may be applied to all learners and are not categorical in nature. A rationale for each factor is given below.

Rate and Amount of Learning Compared to Age Peers

Although learning rate is relative, this factor may be considered as an indication of intellectual ability. Intellectual functioning influences the kind and amount of mathematics the child can learn. Research shows that arithmetic reasoning involving reading and problem-solving develops more slowly than arithmetic fundamentals (Dunn 1973, p. 148).

Speed of Learning Related to Specific Content

Children's acquisition of content that is dependent upon verbal comprehension, perceptual organization and numerical reasoning will vary according to the nature of the task and the individual child.

Ability to Retain Information

Without prerequisite ideas being remembered, new learning is particularly difficult due to the hierarchical nature of mathematics.

Need for Repetition

Many students need a great deal of practice to consolidate their learning. In mathematics, practice should follow meaningful learning. Rote learning that results from premature drill should be guarded against.

Verbal Skills

Mathematical language is embedded in general language and represents symbolic communication in its most basic form. Children who have difficulties using general language symbols often encounter problems with equations and mathematical terminology.

Ability to Learn Arbitrary Associations and Symbol Systems

The child's ability to abstract underlies comprehending the mathematical symbol system.

Size of Vocabulary Compared with Peers

An indication of a child's ability to conceptualize may be found by comparing his vocabulary to that of peers. Cultural and experiential limitations are factors when examining the child's vocabulary.

Ability to Form Relationships, Concepts, and Generalizations

Generalizations are comprised of relating two or more concepts. Examples of the hierarchical nature of mathematics are shown in Figure 8.1.

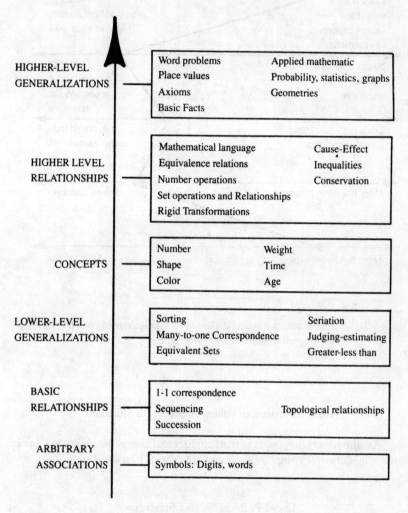

HIGHER-LEVEL GENERALIZATIONS	Word problems · Place values · Axioms · Basic Facts · Applied mathematic · Probability, statistics, graphs · Geometries
HIGHER LEVEL RELATIONSHIPS	Mathematical language · Equivalence relations · Number operations · Set operations and Relationships · Rigid Transformations · Cause-Effect · Inequalities · Conservation
CONCEPTS	Number · Shape · Color · Weight · Time · Age
LOWER-LEVEL GENERALIZATIONS	Sorting · Many-to-one Correspondence · Equivalent Sets · Seriation · Judging-estimating · Greater-less than
BASIC RELATIONSHIPS	1-1 correspondence · Sequencing · Succession · Topological relationships
ARBITRARY ASSOCIATIONS	Symbols: Digits, words

Figure 8.1. Cognitive levels of learning mathematics, from Reisman and Kauffman (1980), p. 11.

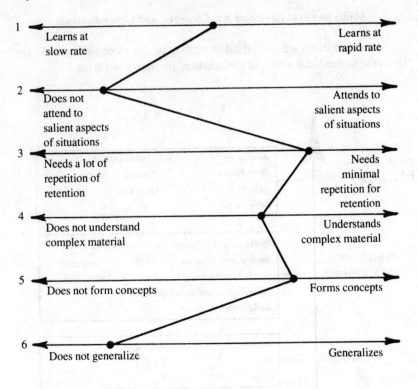

Figure 8.2. A student with a learning disability — average rate of cognitive development, adapted from Reisman (1981), p. 6.

Ability to Attend to Salient Aspects of a Situation

An important component in mathematics learning is the ability to hone in on the relevant while disregarding irrelevant aspects of a situation.

Use of Problem-Solving Strategies

Problem solving, a skill that enhances ability to find solutions, may be learned in a systematic manner. Learning disabled students often rely upon trial and error methods and need to learn problem solving strategies.

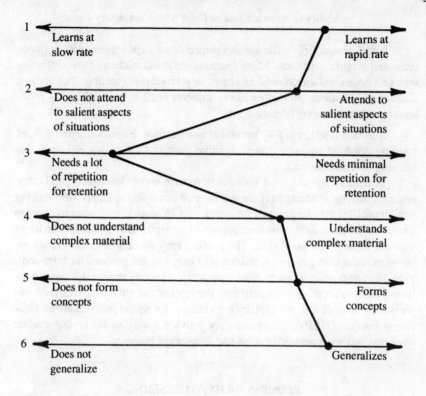

Figure 8.3.   A gifted student with a learning disability — rapid rate of cognitive development, adapted from Reisman (1981), p. 7.

Ability to Make Decisions and Judgments

Children must be able to evaluate situations and make appropriate choices among alternatives.

Ability to Draw Inferences and Conclusions, and to Hypothesize

These abilities are sophisticated skills and need to be specifically provided for during instruction.

Ability to Abstract and to Cope with Complexity

Initial abstracting skills are developed from experiences utilizing concrete and picture activities. Many learning disabled students have difficulty with text pages that are colorful and busy, or with learning settings that involve distracting situations. In mathematics, students need help in analyzing problems to reduce the level of complexity.

Reisman (1981, pp. 6-8) presented two profiles, Figures 8.2 and 8.3, of learning disabled students using cognitive generic factors that influence the learning of mathematics.

Teachers may use these profiles in several ways. Inter-individual comparisons among students may be made. For example, students who exhibit similar profiles may be grouped for instruction. A teacher may want to develop groups in which students who have particular strengths are combined with those who are weak in the same skill. The profiles may serve as a guide for formulating mathematics groups. A teacher also may use the profiles for intra-individual analyses assessing a particular student's strengths and weaknesses. Analyzing an individual's profile may help the teacher use strengths to circumvent weakness. In addition, the profiles are valuable for use in Individualized Education Program (IEP) staffings as they provide a way of observing student strengths and weaknesses for short and long-range planning.

PROCESS OF HYPOTHESIZING

Hypotheses are inferences that serve as a bridge for focusing attention on the relationship between observed strengths and weaknesses and instructional objectives.

PROCESS OF FORMULATING GOALS AND OBJECTIVES

Basing behavioral objectives on the identification and hypothesizing processes enables the teacher to choose tasks and concepts that are matched to the student's functioning. The behavioral objectives serve as a structure for planning curriculum choices and teaching strategies. Stating goals and objectives for learning disabled students provides the teacher with direction for instruction.

PROCESS OF INSTRUCTION

This process involves implementing instructional procedures for learning disabled students. It is based on observations and inferences concerning the student and goals or objectives that were selected for the student. Instructional strategies have emerged from generic learning factors as exhibited by students (see profiles previously presented). Excerpts from profiles will be used as examples for the basis of instruction. Teaching strategies are taken from Reisman & Kauffman (1980).

A Student with a Learning Disability — Average Rate of Cognitive Development.

Learns at slow rate

Learns at rapid rate

This student shows average rate of learning compared to age peers. No special strategies. Same as for "average" learners.

Does not attend to salient aspects of situations

Attends to salient aspects of situations

Student has difficulty attending to salient aspects of a situation.

Suggested Teaching Strategies

Present small amounts; chunking

Separate the components of simple directions into small bits. For example, modify the directions "Count out loud until I say 'STOP' to "Count one, two." Then after the child does this, proceed with the direction "Count one, two, three" (p. 53).

Use visual or auditory cues that highlight the position of an item in a sequence

This approach sometimes facilitates learning the entire sequence. Examples include writing in a different color or on a different background the digit whose position is either first in a series or in the middle (p. 54).

Use separating and underlining as cues

Present a span of digits in either of the following ways to incorporate separating and/or underlining as aids to memory (p. 55).

123   456   789

123456789;   123456789;   123456789

Control number of dimensions that define a linear sequence

If the student is expected to sequence by length, then straws, rods, and so forth should differ only in length. Do not introduce different colors, textures, or widths into initial sequencing-by-length tasks; that is, omit features irrelevant to the linear sequence (p. 55).

Point out relevant relationships

To help students construct the relationships of proximity, enclosure, and separateness it is important to isolate the relationships. A student may be unable to discover a particular relationship because he attends to unrelated aspects. Therefore, you must point out what is near to an object and far away from another. Use a minimum of words — omit extraneous words in helping students to see these spatial relationships. For example:

> Mary near desk (proximity)
> John inside tire (enclosure)
> Puzzle apart. Put together. (separateness) (p. 64).

<----------------------------------•------->

Needs a lot of		Needs minimal
repetition for		repetition for
retention		retention

Student needs minimal repetition for retention. No special strategies needed.

Be aware that this student will not need very much repetition in order to retain the information.

Does not understand
complex material

Understands
complex material

This student is slightly above the average in understanding complex material.

Suggested Instructional Strategies

Provide sequencing activities comprised of more complex or subtle nature

Torrance suggests ordering "sequencing of events in cartoons, photographs, . . . events in creative dramatics, the daily schedule" (p. 58).

Increase complexity of tasks

When ordering objects, provide opportunities for students to practice comparatives that express asymmetric, transitive relationships: This straw is next because it's longer than that one, but shorter than those (p. 85).

Does not form
concepts

Forms
concepts

Students is above average in ability to form concepts.

Suggested Instructional Strategies

Increase task complexity

Use of logic or attribute blocks presents a challenging series of conceptualizations for students with above average ability to form concepts. An example of an attribute block activity would be the following: Using blue, red, and yellow triangles of two thicknesses, say, "Make groups such that something is the same about all the things within a group." Then change the objects. Introducing different properties described, provide new categories (p. 96).

Does not   Generalizes
generalize

Student is below average in the ability to generalize.

Suggested Instructional Strategies

Control the number of dimensions embedded in the stimuli

Provide students with a set of three pennies and ask him to make another set to match the original pennies. Then, as students are able to perform this task, introduce an additional attribute that is irrelevant to constructing equivalence of groups. Thus, if red blocks were used, give students blue, green, or yellow blocks (p. 76).

Restrict complexity of incidental learning to the gross and obvious

Provide situations involving matching of groups where large differences in number occur. For example, have too few chairs at the table for the number of students who must sit, too few lunches one day so some have to wait for theirs; or too many tickets to a movie so they can invite some friends to go too (p. 78).

Use the familiar and useful

Provide students with objects that are familiar to them and preferably useful. The following are examples used for sorting tasks:

money: coins or paper bills
buttons: round or not round, two holes or four holes, plastic or wooden
clothes: hot weather or cold weather

Use of verbalization by model

A model is seated next to students and states the steps they need for seriation: "I will order these blocks by size. I put the smallest here, and the biggest over here (as the task is being performed). Then I find the one closest in size to the smallest. Then I put this one next — it's a little bigger, then the next bigger . . . " (p. 87).

Emphasize patterns

Patterns are particularly appropriate for helping students to see which numbers are components of a larger number. Patterns may be shown at both the concrete and picture levels. Patterns may be emphasized by using playing cards, dominoes, and grids.

A Gifted Student with a Learning Disability — Rapid Rate of Cognitive Development (Reisman & Kauffman 1980)

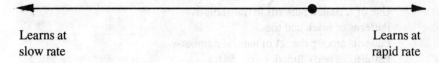

Learns at	Learns at
slow rate	rapid rate

This student learns at a much faster rate than the "average student."

Suggested Instructional Strategy

Introduce novelty into learning experiences

This activity is particularly appropriate for the creatively gifted student, since the strategy allows for new and original relationships. An example is to have students generate sentences from a thinking square. The thinking square is a four-by-four square containing 16 words, which can be grouped to generate 256 sentences (p. 129).

Does not attend	Attends to
to salient aspects	salient aspects
of situations	of situations

Student is above average in ability to attend to salient aspects of situations. No special strategies needed.

Needs a lot of	Needs minimal
repetition for	repetition for
retention	retention

Although this student learns at a faster cognitive rate, he or she needs more repetition for retention than the "average student" his or her age.

Suggested Instructional Strategies

Emphasize patterns that generate the sequence

Use of dominoes to teach number sequence.
Use of repeated patterns in translations.
Patterns of brick and tiles.
Patterns among the set of natural numbers.
Patterns in body functions (p. 56).

Teach use of rehearsal strategies

Mercer and Snell listed rehearsal strategies that included the following:
   use of cumulative rehearsal (that is, rote repetition — either aloud or
   silently — of increasing stimuli including naming the current visual
   stimulus and then rehearsing three times in sequence all previous
   items plus the current item)
visual imagery strategies (such as use of mental pictures)
repetition
verbal elaboration
systematic scanning and pointing
cue selection (for example, use of color or some other dimension of
   a stimulus)
chunking (for example, grouping of material, as in a number series
   (pp. 56-57).

Emphasize differences in distinctive features of stimuli

An example of this is pointing out that for basic multiplication facts with the number 9 as one factor, the sum of the digits of any multiple of 9 is 9. Another distinctive feature of the relationship among basic facts involving 9 is that in the table of nines (for facts greater thn $0 \times 9 = 0$), the tens digit increases by one as the units digit decreases by one.

$1 \times 9 = 9$	$\longrightarrow 0 + 9 = 9$
$2 \times 9 = 18$	$\longrightarrow 1 + 8 = 9$
$3 \times 9 = 27$	$\longrightarrow 2 + 7 = 9$
$4 \times 9 = 36$	$\longrightarrow 3 + 6 = 9$
$5 \times 9 = 45$	$\longrightarrow 4 + 5 = 9$
$6 \times 9 = 54$	$\longrightarrow 5 + 4 = 9$
$7 \times 9 = 63$	$\longrightarrow 6 + 3 = 9$
$8 \times 9 = 72$	$\longrightarrow 7 + 2 = 9$
$9 \times 9 = 81$	$\longrightarrow 8 + 1 = 9$

This is an example of how this teaching strategy may be used as a check for correctness of products. Other applications may serve to highlight such distinctive features as form, color, functions, and so on when constructing higher-level generalizations. For example, "all round things roll," "red on traffic lights means stop," "sharp edges cut."

It is important that the teacher develop patterns such as this with caution. Unless students are constructing the patterns, they may become confused with such patterns or shortcuts. Students should not be left with a jumble of short rules that they cannot tie to a foundation. Some use of patterns is helpful, especially in aiding retention; however, do not become carried away stressing these to a student (p. 140).

$\longleftarrow$————————●————————$\longrightarrow$

Does not understand   Understands
complex material   complex material

Student is above average in ability to understand complex material, as was the student in Profile 1. Teaching strategies would be similar.

$\longleftarrow$————————●————————$\longrightarrow$

Does not   Forms
form concepts   concepts

Student is above average in ability to form concepts, as was student in Profile 1. See Profile 1 for suggested teaching strategy.

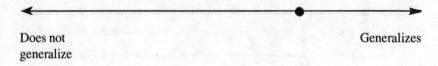

Does not
generalize

Generalizes

Student is above average in ability to generalize.

Suggested Instructional Strategies

Use Reisman computation board

An adaptation of the R-K counting board is the Reisman computation board (Figure 8.4), in which the spaces are reduced from nine to four by utilizing the duality idea. The four spaces have doubles values (ones place, twos, fours, eights) (Reisman & Kauffman 1980, pp. 146-47).

8
4
2
1

Figure 8.4. Reisman computation board.

The Reisman computation board is a vehicle for investigating basic facts. It is a more abstract procedure and may be more appropriate for those students developing at a rapid cognitive rate. Each space has a value. A token placed on a space represents one of the space's value.

Using the many-to-one idea, tell students to make a two-for-one exchange in order to move from one space to the next higher. In making the two-for-one exchange, some students cannot go directly from space one to space two. They need to exchange their two "space one" tokens for a third token and then place that on space two.

Tell students to identify all the ways they can show a number on a board. You might wish to have several boards available so that all combinations of a number may be shown. Figure 8.5 shows the number 4 in different ways. Note that the basic fact which is not apparent, *3 + 1*, may be obtained by applying the associative or grouping property.

$$[(1 + 1) + 1] + 1 \text{ or } (2 + 1) + 1.$$

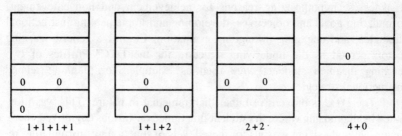

Figure 8.5. Use of Reisman computation board.

Provide both verbal-logical and visual-pictorial tasks

Some students may be able to find the generalization or principle that underlies a numerical series but have difficulty with spatial arrangement of elements. Therefore, provide both types of tasks. This information may be used for identifying the students' strengths and weaknesses. The student who is less able to do numerical sequence may be displaying syntactic disability and may have difficulty in algebra. Those who cannot perform the figural tasks may have difficulty with geometry, which is spatial. Teaching to a student's strengths is important in curriculum selection. If your purpose is for the student to generate series, then be sure the tasks involve examples that relate to his strength.

PROCESS OF ONGOING EVALUATION

The ongoing nature of *evaluation* is very important in providing for feedback on the student as well as on the mathematics program. Evaluating the original hypotheses and objectives must be done throughout the diagnostic cycle. The original objectives may be modified, enlarged upon or discarded as determined by the information derived from assessment. In essence, evaluation takes on both a summative and a formative role in the diagnostic teaching cycle.

Formative evaluation occurs throughout the process of instruction. Student gains should be continuously noted, just as student difficulties must guide planning. Summative evaluation occurs after instruction. Information gathered at this time provides feedback for further planning.

SUMMARY

The Diagnostic Teaching Cycle (Reisman 1982), has been explained in terms of the educational needs of learning disabled students in mathematics. The DTC involves five processes which were discussed: identifying strengths and weaknesses, hypothesizing reasons for achievement and nonachievement, formulating goals and objectives, developing and implementing instructional strategies, and engaging in ongoing evaluation. Cognitive generic learning factors served as the underlying structure for the DTC. Profiles of two learning disabled students were used as examples for planning related instructional strategies.

The DTC is preventive rather than remedial in nature. This was illustrated by diagnosing where the student functioned on various cognitive generic factors, hypothesizing reasons for these levels of functioning, formulating related goals and objectives, providing instruction aimed at students' strengths, and evaluating throughout the cycle. Instructional strategies were based on students' profiles, reflected learning strengths and were geared toward circumventing weakness.

It is crucial that learning disabled students experience success situations (Love 1972, pp. 186-187). Employing the Diagnostic Teaching Cycle, which focuses on facilitating strengths and circumventing weaknesses, insures this sense of success for students with learning disabilities.

REFERENCES

Dunn, M. *Exceptional Children in the Schools — Special Education in Transition*, 2nd ed. New York: Holt, Rinehart & Winston, 1973.

Love, H. D. *Educating Exceptional Children in Regular Classrooms*. Springfield, Ill.: Thomas, 1972.

Payne, D. A., and R. F. McMorris. *Education and Psychological Measurement: Contributions to Theory and Practice*, 2nd ed. Morristown, N.J.: General Learning Press, 1975.

Reisman, F. K. *Teaching Mathematics: Methods and Content*. Dallas, Tex.: Houghton Mifflin, 1981.

——, *A Guide to the Diagnostic Teaching of Arithmetic*, 3rd ed. Columbus, Oh.: Charles E. Merrill, 1982.

——, and S. H. Kauffman. *Teaching Mathematics to Children with Special Needs*. Columbus, Oh.: Charles E. Merrill, 1980.

9

Class Size Limits and Weighting Formulae
A Crucial Issue in the Mainstreaming Movement

Paul J. Gerber

As the practice of mainstreaming handicapped children and youth into regular classrooms establishes itself as a norm within the educational arena, the often-debated issue of class size takes on new dimensions. The infusion of special needs individuals into the mainstream poses interesting questions that must be studied by regular and special educators alike. The issue of central importance focuses on limits for regular class size, and weighting commensurate to disability category when exceptional students are mainstreamed. Although the general inclination of those who advocate for handicapped students is to reject this concept at face value, it may have to be addressed by the educational community in the not too distant future.

CONFLUENT TRENDS

There are a number of confluent trends that underscore the momentum of this issue. Though the passage of PL 94-142, federal law has mandated a free, appropriate education for all handicapped students. Subsequently, vigorous child find efforts have sought full implementation of the law and have identified significant numbers of handicapped children needing special educational services. Despite the growing numbers of exceptional students few have argued with their fundamental birthright.

The mandate for educational placement in the least restrictive environment has fueled the movement of mainstreaming; but this is matched only by the logic of financial management within the nation's public schools. The practice of mainstreaming may make sound educational sense, but it has become an important fiscal tool for school district administrators. In the current economic climate of spiraling inflation and weakened tax bases, the costs of special educational services pose a pressing problem. The National School Boards Association (1979) has highlighted the dilemma:

—The local education agency budgets for special education are rising at 14% per year or twice as rapidly as instructional and operating budgets of 7-8% per year.

—The cost ratio between education of the handicapped and regular education is at least 2:1 nationwide (thought to be a conservative estimate).
—Out of an average per pupil cost of $3,638 annually for handicapped students, the federal government will be contributing only slightly over $200 per child (average per pupil expenditure in FY 1980 is $1,819).

As part of the increased emphasis on mainstreaming, both programmatically and financially, the United States Office of Civil Rights reports significantly more handicapped individuals are being educated in the regular classroom (*Spectrum* 1980). This has increased teacher load with a student who places increased demands on the regular classroom teacher. In lieu of this trend, it has now become apparent that weighting the count of handicapped children and setting ceilings for regular class size will become important issues.

THE ISSUE OF CLASS SIZE

Class size vis-a-vis handicapping condition or diagnostic category has been mandated by state special education laws. In order to insure quality programming, maximum numbers of students have been set for self-contained classes and special resource room instruction. Typically, the greater the degree of severity, the lower the teacher-student ratio. Moreover, funding and reimbursement practices had been predicated on these ratios.

On the other hand, there have never been legally mandated class sizes in the regular education sector. Exhaustive studies have been undertaken to assess the relationship between class size and achievement. Yet results are inconclusive due to methodological problems. This leaves one able to champion both sides of the issue. However, it is argued that smaller classes decrease teacher stress, increase morale, allow for greater student-teacher contact and facilitate small group instruction. Haddad (1978) reports in a review of the literature that teachers believe a maximum of 30 students to be the "breaking point" while a National Education Association study found two-thirds of respondents favored class size not to exceed 24.

The crossover placement between special education/regular education lines subsequently intensifies the question of class size. When a handicapped individual enters a regular classroom, the class size restrictions of the diagnostic category are no longer valid. This theoretically enables *unlimited numbers* of handicapped students in any given regular class. Yet this is without added *in-class* help for regular education teachers who must educate handicapped individuals with diverse learning, behavioral, psychological and physical needs, along with numerous other nonhandicapped students. This creates a situation in which handicapped and nonhandicapped children both may suffer because of the excess demands in the classroom where mainstreaming is practiced.

Two school districts, Denver, Colorado, and Lodi, California, have implemented a system of weights apropos to class size in the mainstreaming situation. This idea has surfaced among educators across the country, but none has addressed the issue as directly as the national and state teachers' unions, which have articulated the issue of class size and mainstreaming handicapped individuals.

POSITIONS OF NATIONAL ORGANIZATIONS

The two national teachers' organizations, the American Federation of Teachers (AFT) and the National Education Association (NEA) have gone on record on the issue of mainstreaming and regular class size. The AFT put forth its initial position prior to the passage of PL 94-142 and modified its stand in subsequent policy resolutions throughout the decade of the 1970s. The NEA proffered its position approximately at the time of the passage of the federal mandatory special education act.

In a 1971 resolution, "Problems Stemming from the Education of Handicapped Act PL 94-142," AFT urged its state and local chapters to negotiate class size reductions when special education pupils are mainstreamed. In addition, they advocated a limit on the number of special education pupils to be included in any specific class.

In 1975, upon the passage of PL 94-142, the national AFT convention passed a resolution supporting the mainstreaming of handicapped children, with certain stipulations. One of them was viable class sizes apropos to the mainstreaming situation.

Subsequent statements of the AFT concerning the practice of mainstreaming reflected greater specificity. A policy statement on "Class Size for Special Education" (1976) reiterated the theme of the 1971 resolution. There was a significant modification, however. The AFT stated "where mainstreaming with regular pupils is involved class size should not exceed the limits established for special education classes." That same year a separate policy statement entitled "Mainstreaming" addressed class reduction "citing specific numbers." It stated that "sound reductions be made in class size, with up to but no more than two handicapped students in a regular class when such type of class situation is involved."

The NEA has also gone on record on the issue of mainstreaming and weighting procedures. As part of a comprehensive policy statement on mainstreaming one component addresses class size. The NEA supports the concept of mainstreaming when "modifications are made in the size of all classes using weighted factors, scheduling, and curriculum designed to accommodate the shifting demands that mainstreaming creates." There is no mention of actual class size limits or specific weighting formulae in their position, however.

POSITIONS OF STATE AFFILIATES

The NEA state affiliates have viewed the modification of regular education class size through weighting factors as highly relevant to the mainstreaming process. In a survey of the NEA state organizations, the majority of affiliates stated this to be the case. A great number of class size positions emanate from the provision of the national NEA stated previously. There are, however, more specific positions on this issue by various affiliates.

The Hawaii State Teachers' Association supports a weighting procedure so that no child will be neglected due to additional instructional responsibilities. This is also true of the Arkansas Educational Association. The New Jersey Education Association calls for a statement of maximum class size of regular classrooms into which handicapped children may be placed, maximum hours during the school day for such placement, and maximum numbers of handi-

Table 9.1

Virginia Education Association Weighting Formula for Mainstreamed Special Education Students

Exceptionality	Minimum Weighting Factor
Deaf	3.0
Deaf/Blind	5.0
Hearing Impaired	2.0
Educable Mentally Retarded	2.0
Trainable Mentally Retarded	4.0
Multihandicapped	4.0
Orthopedically Handicapped	4.0
Other Health Impaired	1.5
Emotionally Disturbed	4.0
Learning Disabled	3.0
Speech Disabled	1.5
Visually Impaired	3.0

capped students for each regular classroom. None of the affiliates suggests weighting factors in their positions, however.

Three state affiliates have delineated weighting schedules for handicapped children when they are mainstreamed in the regular classroom. Table 9.1 shows the Virginia Education Association weighting formula. It is implemented if a special education student spends at least one hour or one instructional period in the regular class. Virginia has weighted according to the perception of severity of disability and has addressed the diagnostic categories traditionally found in mandatory special education laws.

The Idaho Education Association puts forth a different weighting schedule from the Virginia affiliate. It differs in two respects. First, it places regular classroom size limits. Moreover, it calls for a maximum of 24 students in grades K-1, 25 students in grades 2-3, 26 students in grades 4-6, and 27 students in grades 7-12. Second, within those limits Idaho puts forth its weighting factors for special education students. Table 9.2 reveals that they have not only weighted for certifiable disability categories but have also included less precisely defined "exceptionalities." Remarkably, they have left out sensorily and orthopedically handicapped students.

In a similar manner, Montana puts forth a weighting formula schedule that is broader than the standard special education diagnostic categories. Their method is similar to their neighbor to the west, Idaho. Yet they include different categories of "exceptional students" while excluding lower functioning men-

Table 9.2
Idaho Education Association Weighting Formula
for Mainstreamed Special Education Students

Exceptionality	Minimum Weighting Factor
Normal	1.0
Gifted/Talented	1.5
Slow Learner	1.5
Bilingual	1.5
Reading Disability	1.5
Transient	1.5
Learning Disabled	2.0
Discipline Problem	2.0
Educable Mentally Retarded	2.0
Educationally Handicapped	2.5
Hyperactive	2.5
Non-English Speaking	2.5
Physically Handicapped	2.5

tally retarded, sensorily handicapped and learning disabled students to name a few. Their oversight of learning disabilities is most notable because of the many learning disabled students who are mainstreamed. Table 9.3 shows the Montana schedule.

Table 9.3
Montana Education Association Weighting Formula
for Mainstreamed Special Education Students

Exceptionality	Minimum Weighting Factor
Normal Functioning	1.0
Fast or Accelerated Learner	1.5
Slow Learner	1.5
Emotionally Disturbed	2.5
Delayed Development	2.0
Educationally Handicapped	2.5
Restless Children	2.5
Bilingual	1.5
Non-English Speaking	2.5
Transient	2.0
Disciplinary Problems	2.0
Resident Dropouts	1.0
Educable Mentally Retarded	2.0

The AFT state affiliates have also taken a stand on the numbers of handicapped children to be mainstreamed into the regular classroom. In contrast to NEA state affiliates, there is not a large number of resolutions in this area. Yet various states have developed their own position through their union mechanisms. Michigan (1978) urges its local affiliates to negotiate contractual safeguards with respect to handicapped children and class size. They do not state absolute numbers, but they favor a reduction of students when special education pupils are mainstreamed. Moreover, they suggest that their local bargaining units limit the number of special education pupils to be included in any regular class.

Louisiana (1978) does not mention class size per se, but suggests that modifications be made in regular class size to accommodate the shifting demands that mainstreaming creates. In contrast to other state positions, Minnesota (1977) sets a numerical limit on class size. It urges collective bargaining agreements to limit the total number of students to twenty counting any exceptional child who may be placed in a regular classroom for any part of the day.

The New York State affiliate (1979) possesses the most comprehensive statement on class size. They address the issue in three ways. First, a weighting factor should be assigned to each handicapped child entering the regular class.

Weight factors depend on severity of handicap. Furthermore, this is extended to specialization areas such as physical education, art, home economics, occupational education, etc.

Second, there should be a limit placed on the number of special students placed in any classroom. Also, no regular class would be permitted to contain more than a certain minor percentage of special students, also using weighting factors. Last, any regular classroom that accepts special education students is assigned a paraprofessional aide. They do not suggest a weighting schedule, however.

DISCUSSION

While the practice of devising differential weights for mainstreaming handicapped students seems to be a remedy for this evergrowing issue, there are problems which arise from a philosophical as well as administrative perspective. Surely, weighting schedules formulated according to diagnostic category are counter to the stated purposes of normalization (Wolfensberger, 1974). Moreover, the implicit notion of inequality does not seem to be in the spirit of PL 94-142 and other legislation which secure rights for handicapped persons.

Yet from an administrative point of view the idea may be a viable option, but inconsistency in logic poses problems in implementation. Theoretically, without a weighting formula for mainstreamed students, a regular classroom may be overloaded with exceptional children. This point is addressed by the New York AFT position which has advocated for handicapped students to be a minor percentage of the regular class. This highlights the possibility of more handicapped students attending a regular class than may be permitted by the class size regulations in state mandatory special education laws.

The proposed weighting schedules raise questions also. The weights assigned to the disability categories seem arbitrary at best. The weighting factors attempt to weight mild handicaps with few regular student equivalents and severe handicaps with greater equivalents. Each handicap is treated as an absolute construct. Currently, there are no formulae which address the continuum of severity that may be found in such diagnostic categories as learning disabilities, sensory handicaps, and orthopedic handicaps. This would create added complexities to this practice.

In addition, the appearance of other categories for weighting reveals the appeal of this practice. The acceptance of weights for handicapped students has set a precedent for the application of weights to other students who pose varying problems to regular classroom instruction.

The nationwide appearance of weighting suggestions for mainstreamed handicapped students indicates an inherent problem within the mainstreaming movement itself. In reality, the weighting of mainstreamed handicapped individuals already exists (though on a small scale). No doubt, the issue will gain prominence with shrinking education dollars and alternative funding procedures. It also promises to be a reoccurring theme as national, state, and local teachers' unions continue to view this as a bargaining issue.

Ultimately, without resolution of this issue education may suffer structurally. The specific effects of mainstreaming unlimited numbers of handicapped students into regular classrooms without added in-class support contributes heavily to teacher stress and ultimate burnout. It becomes a divisive issue in the regular education/special education partnership in educating handicapped students in the least restrictive environment. Moreover, it impairs the qualitative elements of the educational process where the situation is abused.

The issue of class size with respect to mainstreaming is an example of an educational development that has fallen "in between the cracks." The situation has developed as the mandates of federal and state laws have impacted on service delivery to handicapped students. The challenge then rests on adaptability and pragmatism in the educational community. Hopefully, this attitude will allow for a solution that will be beneficial for all parties involved in the mainstreaming process.

REFERENCES

American Federation of Teachers. *Class Size for Special Education Policy Resolution*. 1976.

American Federation of Teachers. *Mainstreaming Policy-Resolution*. 1976.

American Federation of Teachers. *Problems Stemming from Education of Handicapped Act P.L. 94-142*. 1971.

Arkansas Education Association. *Education of Handicapped Children*. November 1979.

Educational Research Service. "Class size research: a critique of recent meta-analyses." *Phi Delta Kappan* (December 1980): 239-241.

Elementary Committee Task Force of the Minnesota Federation of Teachers. *Mainstreaming Position Paper*. October 1977.

Haddad, Wadi D. *Educational Effects of Class Size*. June 1978, *ERIC*, No. 179003.

Hawaii Education Association. *Implementation of P.L. 94-142: Weighted Count of Handicapped Children Resolution XV*, 1979.

Idaho Education Association. *Class Size Policy Statement*. 1979.

——. "Mainstreaming Makes Inroads in Schools." *Spectrum* (publication of the AFT Teachers' Network for the Education of the Handicapped) 2, No. 2 (February 1981).

Michigan Federation of Teachers. *Education of the Handicapped on the Least Restrictive Environment*. Appendix C, Resolution number 5. May 1979.

National Education Association. *Resolution B-25 Education for All Handicapped Children*. September 10, 1980.

National School Boards Association. *A Survey of Special Education Costs in Local School Districts*. Washington, D.C., 1979.

New Jersey Education Association. *Policy Statement on Mainstreaming*. January 22, 1977.

New York State United Teachers' Task Force on Mainstreaming. *Policy Statement on Mainstreaming*. October 21, 1979.

Shanker, Albert. *Testimony of the President of American Federation of Teachers, AFL-CIO, to the Senate Subcommittee on the Handicapped on P.L. 94-142*. July 31, 1980.

United Teachers of New Orleans. *Resolution 15*. October 1979.

Virginia Education Association. *Resolution 80-1*. 1980.

Wolfensberger, W. *Normalization*. Toronto: Canadian National Institute for Mental Health, 1974.

10

Considerations for Training Programs for Parents of Exceptional Children

Janice R. Duncan

W ITH THE PASSAGE of the Education for All Handicapped Children Act of 1975 (Public Law 94-142), provisions were mandated for involvement of parents in planning and participating in the educational programs of their handicapped children. The Rules and Regulations of this Act (Federal Register, 1977) specify that provisions for "participation and consultation" with parents of handicapped children in the development of their child's educational program must be provided. Other sections within the Rules and Regulations deal with the inclusion of parents as members of the team that develops the individualized education program. The Act also provides safeguards that insure the protection of parents' rights. Throughout the Rules and Regulations, parents are included as one of the groups to which the various legal requirements are directed. Now, the question of parental involvement is not *"whether* families should be included but *how* they should be most effectively involved" (Bricker and Casuso 1979, p. 108). The Rules and Regulations of the Act also stipulate that for effective involvement in individualized education program conferences *all* individuals involved should be prepared to have *informed* participation. But how are parents to become informed? How can they learn the esoteric vocabulary that is typically used whenever two or more special education professionals meet? How can parents make a genuine contribution to the planning and implementation of educational programs for their child? These questions appear to be related to the limited involvement in educational planning and participation on the part of some parents and reflect the need for parent training programs.

PARENT INVOLVEMENT

Although Public Law 94-142 requires that provisions be afforded to parents for full participation in planning their child's educational program, the degree of parental contribution to decisions reached at individualized education program meetings appears questionable. Gilliam (1979) conducted a study to determine the perceived rank order of personnel involved in educational planning meetings and the actual contribution of the personnel. The perceived rank order status of 15 roles representative of participants most often included in educational planning meetings was obtained prior to actual meetings. After the meeting the participants evaluated the actual contributions of the individuals involved. Data indicated that parents were rated high in perceived importance prior to the meetings but lower in relation to their actual contributions. Gilliam suggested that while parents are viewed as important because of their close contact with the child, their actual contributions may be limited because of feelings of "intimidation." These feelings may be explained by the lack of parental familiarity with terminology used to report information about test scores, cumulative records, and diagnostic reports. This lack of familiarity limits the parents' understanding and, hence, limits their contributions in these areas.

Lack of actual parental involvement also was indicated in a study by Kirp, Buss, and Kuriloff (1974) who found that, in the majority of school districts investigated, the formal education planning meeting where parents were involved only served to provide endorsement of previously made decisions. Similarly, a study of about 1300 professional members of educational planning teams (Yoshida, Fenton, Kaufman, and Maxwell 1978) indicated that parents were viewed primarily as "gatherers and presenters of information" rather than actual contributors to the educational planning for their children. It well may be that school personnel encourage parent participation only at an informal or non-meaningful level. The model parent has been described as one "who neither resists nor discusses" but complies with the professionals' decisions (Kirp et al. 1974, p. 105). However, examination of Public Law 94-142 reveals that parent involvement is intended to be more than superficial endorsement of professional opinions. Public Law 94-142 recognizes that any individual who is required to participate in the education of handicapped children under the specifications of this mandate might, indeed, need additional training. The Rules and Regulations for an important section of Public Law 94-142, the comprehensive system of personnel development, specify that areas must be identified where training needs exist and appropriate inservice training must be provided (Federal Register, 1977). Parents of handicapped children are included as one of the groups which might need such training. Thus, Public Law 94-142 not only requires participation, consultation, and involvement of parents, but includes the requirement of identification of the need for possible parent training and the provision for such training, when needed.

The legal requirement for the provision of training, where needed, and recognition of the importance of the role of parents in the child's learning have resulted in an increase in the interest in parental training programs and in identifying the factors which contribute to the effectiveness of these programs. A national survey by Schofer and Duncan (1980) found that of the respondents who identified the groups within their state who need training, parents were ranked by 63 percent of the states as one of the first five groups needing training. Only two other groups were listed more frequently. This is similar to the results found by Rude (1978) in a study of State's Annual Program Plan (APP) (now called State Plans) which found that parents were identified in the highest priority group needing to be trained. "Implementing Public Law 94-142" and "individualized education programs" were listed as the two most important training topics for parents. However, actual provision of parent training appears to be less than optimal (Schuck 1979).

PARENT TRAINING PROGRAMS

Programs designed to provide training for parents of handicapped children include those which train parents to take an active and direct role as change agents in the child's cognitive or behavioral activities, those which teach the parent to provide a more effective learning environment in the home, and those which merely include parents in a "helper" or observer capacity where a parent participates in an occasional classroom activity. Training may be based in the home, school, clinic, or hospital where it is delivered on a class, small group, family, or individual basis (Hickey, Imber, and Ruggiero 1979; Johnson and Katz 1973; McWilliams and Cunningham 1976; Wilton 1975). However, one factor common to most programs is a need for a more systematic approach in developing programs for helping parents take an active role in their child's educational program (Baker 1976; Karnes and Zehrbach 1975; Pysh and Chalfant 1978). An examination by Johnson and Katz (1973) of thirty-one studies reporting on programs which used parents as change agents in modifying their child's undesirable behavior found that only slightly more than one-third of the studies included adequate descriptions of the parent training operations and less than one-third provided any estimate of the program's reliability. A similar analysis of parent-intervention programs by Levitt and Cohen (1975) found that over one-half of the parent training programs for the handicapped did not use any evaluative measures and that many of these programs were designed less carefully than programs for disadvantaged children. Levitt and Cohen concluded that most parent-intervention programs for the handicapped were informal and less comprehensive than desirable and recommended that a more rigorous approach be utilized in the programs' structure. As the critical importance of family involvement has become recognized, Karnes and Zehrbach (1975) noted the interest of varying groups, e.g., teachers, lawyers, and social workers, and their differing emphasis on various training topics including legal aspects, educational goals, and social problems; however, these authors noted that this interest and involvement lacked a systematic structure or approach.

McWirter (1976) described a parent education procedure used to provide parents with a survey of information about learning disabilities. The purpose in this program was to provide increased factual knowledge about learning disabilities to parents in order to decrease anxiety and improve the effectiveness of the parents as teachers of their learning disabled children. This program had designated content presented during six sessions; however, the prior knowledge of the participants apparently was not considered. The author noted that the family who left the group had attended a college learning disabilities course and felt that the information presented would be repetitious. This implies that no assessment of the existing knowledge of the participating parents was made. Often, the descriptions of the parent training program indicate that each planning session may be well-organized and appropriately designed to aid the parent in understanding the child's learning problem, but the program usually lacks any predetermination of parental knowledge and/or needs and utilizes no final assessment to determine the impact of the training.

Various models for systematic parental involvement have been proposed. While parent-teacher meetings and training sessions have had some beneficial results, structured programs which have a component for identification of parental needs and have provisions for matching the training to those needs, are seen as necessary to provide a beneficial approach to parent training (Karnes and Zehrbach 1975; Pysh and Chalfant 1978; Stephens 1974; Warfield 1975). Pysh and Chalfant (1978) suggested that training programs for parents of learning disabled children should be designed to meet varying parental needs because the parents' willingness to participate in the training and parental understanding of learning problems will differ. Similarly, Karnes and Zehrbach (1975) emphasize the importance of designing parent training so that consideration is given to the individual needs of each child, the parents' understanding of these needs, and the parents' abilities. Their eleven-stage model provides for varying degrees of parental involvement at different levels of the program based on the assessed needs of both the parents and the child.

NECESSARY FACTORS

Several factors can be identified as important factors in designing appropriate parent training programs. However, just as there is no ONE reading approach which will prove successful with every child, there is no ONE approach or model which can assure the successful development of parent training programs. Even when specific factors can be identified as important in designing parent training programs, these factors still must be implemented and interpreted appropriately or parent training programs become mere token compliance exercises.

A list of some basic factors important to designing a training program for parents would include the following:

1. Determine the needs
2. Analyze the needs and identify their priority
3. Match the training sessions to the needs identified as priorities
4. Evaluate the outcome

Admittedly, this looks only at minimum components, but examination of possible pitfalls with these four components can illustrate the type of problems encountered in designing parent training programs.

Determine the Needs

This may be done through elaborate, multifaceted standardized assessments; by informal, open-ended questionnaires or surveys; or even through subjective decisions of one or two individuals considered as authorities on the issues. Regardless, the needs assessment is going to be based on a series of decisions beginning with decisions on the type of collection strategy to use, and including numerous decisions regarding who to assess about what. To some degree each of these decisions will influence the information that is ultimately collected. Recognizing the impact the initial decisions can have on the ultimate decisions can contribute to designing a needs assessment that will reflect, more accurately, the true state of the art. For example, including only questions regarding legal rights of parents on the needs assessment will not identify concerns in other areas, e.g., lack of understanding of terminology; emotional conflict over acceptance of the child's handicap; negative attitudes toward school personnel. Similarly, administration of the needs assessment may give a biased view of the true situation. For example, giving the needs assessment only to parents who are members of organizations such as the Association for Children and Adults with Learning Disabilities or National Association for Retarded Citizens does not reflect the view of parents who are not involved in such organizations.

These are just a few of the possible pitfalls associated with determining needs. There are many guidelines for needs assessment which emphasize that determining the need is not a simple question and answer exercise (Chalfant, Duncan, Meyen, Schofer, and Ueberle 1981; *Discrepancy Digest* 1981).

Analyze the Needs and Identify Their Priority

Determining the importance of the identified need may require assessment of other factors. Feelings of intimidation may be identified as a factor limiting parent involvement. Additional assessment may be necessary to determine what needs should be addressed so that this feeling can be modified. Ranking the importance of identified needs on the number of responses would simplify this process. The greatest need would be the one which the most respondents indicated as a concern, however, this ignores other factors which may reflect an essential need for a small group of parents. It also may reflect a "want" rather than a need. Analyzing the need and determining its importance requires knowledge of other factors affecting the situation.

Match the Training Sessions to the Priority Needs

Although this statement may appear axiomatic; obviously, once the need has been identified appropriate training should be provided. However, decisions must be made about what training would be appropriate. A needs assessment may have determined that the lack of parental involvement in planning educational programs for their handicapped child is largely due to limited understanding of the terminology used by the professionals at planning conferences. A training session to provide parents with an understanding of professional jargon could be designed to meet this need. Undoubtedly, a basic primer course for parents on initials commonly used (IEPs, FAPE, MR, MNH, BD, WISC-R, ad nauseam), acronyms, and professional terms could clarify much of what is discussed in these meetings. But this approach must be a continually repeated exercise for parents new to the system, for parents of recently identified handicapped children and for up-dating parents on the ever-changing jargon. The success of this approach is highly dependent on parent participation. Another approach would be to recognize that the need could be ameliorated through modification of the professionals. Providing training sessions for the professionals designed to help them express themselves in clear, concise, generally understood terminology might be much more efficient and effective then providing training for parents.

Numerous other factors must be considered in matching training to needs, including the type of training and delivery (lecture, experiential, modeling, etc.); time and place; needs of participants (child-care services, transportation); trainers; incentives; present level of understanding; individual learning rates. These factors indicate the importance of *individualizing* for parents just as *individualizing* is recommended for students.

Evaluate the Outcome

Ideally, evaluation should be built into the training program from the beginning so that changes can be implemented as needed. Too often, evaluation is an after-the-fact activity conducted to justify the expenditure or to comply with outside regulations. Continuing evaluation can be used to identify problems as they occur and allows for modification so that the final outcomes can be positive. Evaluation can be used to assess the present effect of the program and can help determine future needs.

SUMMARY

It is evident that programs for helping parents assume an active role in planning their child's education program are increasing. We hope these programs will be designed to meet the needs of parents so that they can become active contributors in the educational planning and implementation of an appropriate education for handicapped children.

The participants at this session of the ACLD Convention were asked to respond to similar questions that have been posed in some of the studies cited in this paper. The respondents (13 parents of learning disabled students, 9 professional educators who were not also parents of learning disabled students, and 2 professionals who were also parents of learning disabled students) noted many of the same problems identified in the studies. When asked to rank various roles as to their importance in attending the Individualized Education Program meeting, the parent was ranked much higher than they were ranked on the importance of their actual contributions to this meeting. The participants in this session explained that they believed most parents feel "out-numbered" in these meetings and have difficulty understanding the terminology and "special education jive" that is often used. The participants were eager to discuss possible methods which could be used to help parents overcome these feelings and to have more active participation in IEP planning. Parent in service programs were seen as a very viable way of providing parents with a better understanding the IEP process and were viewed as a way of helping parents overcome the two extremes of either giving a blanket endorsement of the professional educators' suggestions or objecting to the program without a full understanding of it.

The participants were also asked to identify the topics they would like addressed in an in service program for parents. Individuals listed information on legal rights and information on terminology and test interpretation as desired topics. Many of the participants voiced a desire for more information on how to initiate parent training programs and many suggested that they felt this might be an important area for their ACLD chapters to address.

REFERENCES

Baker, B. "Parent involvement in programming for developmentally disabled children." In *Communication assessment and intervention strategies*, edited by L. Lloyd. Baltimore, Md.: University Park Press, 1976.

Bricker, D., and V. Casuso. "Family involvement: A critical component of early intervention." *Exceptional Children* 46 (1979): 108-116.

Chalfant, J., J. Duncan, E. Meyen, R. Schofer, and J. Ueberle. *Comprehensive System of Personnel Development: Needs Assessment Considerations*. Columbia, Mo.: University of Missouri, Columbia, Department of Special Education, June 1981.

Federal Register. Tuesday, August 23, 1977, 42.

Gilliam, J.E. "Contributing and status rankings of educational planning committee participants." *Exceptional Children* 45 (1979): 466-468.

Hickey, K., S. Imber, and E. Ruggiero. "Modifying reading behavior of elementary special needs children: A cooperative resource-parent program. *Journal of Learning Disabilities* 12 (1979): 444-449.

Johnson, C., and R. Katz. "Using parents as change agents for their children: A review." *Journal of Child Psychology and Psychiatry* 14 (1973): 181-200.

Karnes, M. and R. Zehrbach. "Matching families and services." *Exceptional Children* 41 (1975): 545-549.

Kirp, D., W. Buss and P. Kuriloff. "Legal reforms of special education: Empirical studies and procedural proposals." *California Law Review* 62 (1974): 40-155.

Levitt, E., and S. Cohen. "An analysis of selected parent-intervention programs for handicapped and disadvantaged children." *The Journal of Special Education* 9 (1975): 345-365.

McWilliams, D., and P. Cunningham. "Project PEP." *The Reading Teacher* 29 (1976): 655-663.

McWirter, J. "A Parent Education Group in Learning Disabilities." *Journal of Learning Disabilities* 9 (1976): 27-31.

"Needs assessment: Improving the improvements." *Discrepancy Digest* 4, No. 9 (1981): 4-5.

Pysh, M., and J. Chalfant. *The Learning Disabilities Manual: Recommended Procedures and Practices*. State Board of Education, Illinois Office of Education, 1978.

Rude, C. "Trends and priorities in inservice training." *Exceptional Children* 45 (1978): 172-178.

Schofer, R., and J. Duncan. *A national survey of comprehensive systems of personnel development: A third status study*. Columbia, Mo.: University of Missouri, Columbia, Department of Special Education, December, 1980.

Schuck, J. "The parent-professional partnership: Myth or reality?" *Education Unlimited* 1, No. 4 (1979): 26-28.

Stephens, J., Jr. "The home learning project: A group consultation model of parent education." *Child Care Quarterly* 3 (1974): 246-254.

Warfield, G. "Mothers of retarded children review a parent education program." *Exceptional Children* 41 (1975): 1975.

Wilton, V. "A mother-helper scheme in the infant school." *Educational Research* 18 (1975): 3-15.

Yoshida, R., K. Fenton, M. Kaufman, and J. Maxwell. "Parental involvement in the special education pupil planning process: The school's perspective." *Exceptional Children* 44 (1978): 531-534.

11

Vocational Education Practices with Secondary School Age Learning Disabled and Mildly Handicapped Students

Paul J. Gerber and Harold C. Griffin

As THE CONCEPTS of adult adjustment and lifelong learning become an important agenda item in the field of learning disabilities, vocational education has taken on added importance. Ultimately, vocational adjustment will be a major contributor to independent living, workplace productivity, and community participation. Pursuant to the federal mandates specifying entitlement to vocational preparation, those who serve learning disabled and mildly handicapped students have begun to set in motion the administrative and programmatic arrngements needed to ensure quality instruction.

Yet at ths time, we see that significant strides must still be taken to integrate the goals of learning disabilities and vocational habilation (Mori 1980). Gerber (1982) has pointed out that there are problems with the process and structure in delivering vocational education services to learning disabled students. Moreover, he points out that this is symptomatic of a lack of a conceptual model synthesizing educational and vocational programming for learning disabled adolescents.

Despite the commentary, to date there has been little data-based analysis describing the current state of the art. Apropos to this development, the authors investigated vocational education practices used with learning disabled and mildly handicapped students. The focus of the survey was the standard components of traditional vocational education programming.

METHODOLOGY

A survey focusing on vocational programming of learning disabled and mildly disabled students was conducted of junior and senior high school special education teachers. Approximately eighty individuals responded to the survey. Because of problems with missing data and ineligible respondents, only 53 teacher questionnaires were used for the study. This group of 53 teachers was composed of 27 junior high school teachers and 26 high school teachers.

The participants in this study represented a wide spectrum of geographical locations. The teachers in the study were from school districts in Texas, Oklahoma, Louisiana, Alabama, Virginia, North Carolina, California, and Colorado. School districts were both urban and rural. Typically, they contained large to moderate-sized school-age populations. One initial problem was whether or not to utilize teachers of learning disabled children or mildly handicapped students in the study. We decided to include teachers of mildly handicapped students at the secondary level to broaden the pool of subjects in the study. This more accurately reflected the vocational education service deliveryto this population.

It was found that the utilization of multi-categorical classes which includes both students with learning disabilities and other mildly handicapping conditions was the most frequently used organization structure at the secondary level. Because both learning disabled and mildly handicapped secondary level programs were included in this study, inferences concerning the interface between the learning disabled population and vocational habilitation may be limited. This limitation, however, may allow a more realistic interpretation concerning vocational service delivery at the secondary level than just focusing on the learning disabilities/vocational habilitation interface.

There were several domains investigated in the study. They were: vocational assessment, prevocational training, vocational training, curriculum, and the individual education program (IEP) as it relates to vocational training.

Statistically, the data from the domains were analyzed through the utilization of the *Statistical Package for the Social Sciences* (SPSS). "Frequencies" and "one-way" sub-programs were utilized in analyzing the data. In addition, a "select-if" procedure was used to separate the responses of junior and senior high school teachers. The "frequencies" sub-program provided a count of the actual responses to a question as well as the percentage of such responses. The "one-way" sub-program indicated if responses of the junior high teachers were statistically different from those of the senior high school teachers. The level of significance chosen was .05. This was measured through the use of a Scheffé post hoc test at the .05 level in combination with the "one-way" sub-program of SPSS. The Scheffé post hoc test was used because it is stricter than other post hoc tests, allows for the examination of all possible combinations of group means, and is more exact even for unequal sized groups.

RESULTS

Vocational Assessment

When asked if vocation assessment services were provided as a matter of routine, respondents from junior high school programs indicated 25 percent yes and 74.1 percent no, while respondents from high school programs replied 26.9 percent yes and 73.1 percent no. Moreover, a question asked who performed the vocational assessment. The data for the responses are included in Table 11.1.

Table 11.1
Providers of Vocational Assessment Services for
Mildly Handicapped Children

	Junior High	High School
Classroom Teacher	14.8%	11.5%
Counselors	40.7%	26.9%
Vocational Teachers	18.7%	38.5%
Other	25.9%	23.1%

The data in Table 11.1 indicate that the majority of vocational testing was done by counselors and vocational educators in secondary school programs. The prime responsibility shifts from the junior to senior high level, however. Counselors are clearly performing more assessmentduties at the junior high level while vocational educators assume the major responsibility at the senior high level. In addition, frequency of vocational assessment was ascertained. At the junior high level 3.7 percent responded every six months, 14.8 percent every year, 0 percent every two years, and 55.6 percent said no set time. Re-

Table 11.2
Assessment Done to Predict Mastery of Vocational Skills

	Yes	No	No Response
Teachers of junior high students	44.5%	37.0%	18.5%
Teachers of senior high students	38.5%	30.8%	30.7%

spondents from senior high programs indicated 0 percent every six months, 15.4 percent every year, 3.8 percent every two years, 30.8 percent no set time, and 50 percent no response.

Despite the apparent lack of assessment, several questions were asked to assess how vocational assessment data are used. One question asked if assessment was done to predict master of vocational skills. The responses of the study participants are indicated in Table 11.2.

The data in Table 11.3 indicate participant responses to the concept of assessment utilized to predict eventual vocational placement.

Table 11.3
Assessment Utilized to Predict Eventual Vocational Placement

	Yes	No	No Response
Teachers of junior high students	33.3%	51.9%	14.8%
Teachers of senior high students	34.6%	23.1%	42.3%

Another question was asked to determine how mildly handicapped students were placed in either a college bound or non-college bound curriculum. The key factor in placement was reading level as junior high teachers responded 51.9 percent and senior high teachers said 50 percent. The second most important factor was resources within the school as junior high teachers selected this criteria 25.9 percent while senior high teachers indicated 30.8 percent. Personnel available did not seem to be a significant factor. Junior high respondents saw this as important 7.4 percent, and senior high respondents gave it a 15.4 percent rating. The data semed to indicate that vocational assessment criteria did not have a bearing on placement.

Finally, respondents were queried to see whether assessment was done to pinpoint individual vocational programming needs. When asked if assessment was done to specify areas of needed vocational development junior high respondents said 33.8 percent yes, 51.9 percent no with 14.8 percent no response. At the senior high level this was done less often: 11.2 percent yes, 38.5 percent no, and 42.3 percent no response.

DOMAIN 2: PREVOCATIONAL TRAINING

In the area of prevocational training, respondents were asked several questions to assess the extent of their programming efforts. When asked if their respective schools had a bona fide prevocational curriculum junior high teachers said 25.9 percent yes, 70.4 percent no, and 3.7 percent had no response. At the senior high level, 34.6 percent responded yes, 61.5 percent said no, and 3.8 percent indicated no response.

Apropos to finding the extent of the prevocational effort, it was asked how much of the instructional day was devoted to prevocational skill development. Generally, responses were quite similar from junior and senior high respondents as indicated in Table 11.4.

Table 11.4
Portion of Day Devoted to Pre-Vocational Skill Development

	None	20%	60%	80%	Over 80%	No Response
Junior High	22.2%	51.9%	3.7%	10%	0%	22.2%
High School	19.2%	53.8%	0%	0%	0%	26.9%

The majority of respondents of both levels of instruction used one-fifth of their instructional day on prevocational skill development.

Respondents were given a close-ended question in order to evaluate the components of prevocational training. *Skills for community participation* showed 25.9 percent in junior high school, 15.4 percent in senior high schools; *general skills training* revealed 33.3 percent in junior high and 34.4 percent in senior high schools; *increased awareness of prerequisites for specific vocations* showed 29.6 percent in junior high programs and 38.5 percent in senior high programs. All others showed very insignificant percentages.

Finally, a question was asked to see whether pre-vocational curricula simulated work environments. Junior high programs responded 37.0 percent yes, 33.3 percent no, and 29.6 percent had no response. Senior high programs indicated 30.8 percent yes, 26.9 percent no with 42.3 percent having no response.

Because career awareness programming is typically mixed in with prevocational programming when educating mildly handicapped students, several questions were asked within the prevocational section pertaining to career awareness. Teachers were asked if their programs included a career awareness program for mildly handicapped students. Junior high teachers said 77.8 percent yes, 18.5 percent no, and 3.7 percent indicated no response. Senior high teachers said 65.4 percent yes, 26.9 percent no and 7.7 percent had no re-

sponse. Moreover, it was asked how this part of the curriculum was implemented. At the junior high level 48.1 percent said it was integrated into the
regular curriculum, 18.5 percent said career awareness was relegated to a specific class, and 33.3 percent said it was part of special education programming
exclusively. At the senior high level the results differed. They were 30.8 percent, 19.2 percent, and 42.3 percent respectively.

DOMAIN 3: VOCATIONAL TRAINING

In the vocational training section of the survey, questions addressed several
different areas. Teachers were asked if mildly handicapped students received
vocational training which differed from that received by nonhandicapped
students. Senior high programs tended to separate the students more. They
responded 38.5 percent yes and 57.7 percent no. Junior high respondents indicated 22.2 percent yes and 77.8 percent no.

Respondents also were asked if mildly handicapped students are mainstreamed into vocational training programs for nonhandicapped students. The
results showed a heavy emphasis on mainstreaming at the junior and senior high
school levels. Junior high teachers responded 81.5 percent yes, 11.1 percent no
and no response 7.4 percent. Similarly, senior high respondents said yes 76.9
percent, no 15.4 percent with 7.7 percent no response.

Another question focused on the development of the vocational curriculum for mildly handicapped students. Specifically, it was asked who designed
the vocational curriculum, and responses showed vocational teachers and special education teachers to have the most involvement. These responses are presented in Table 11.5.

Table 11.5
**Personnel Responsible for the Design of Vocational Curriculum for
Mildly Handicapped Students**

	Junior High	High School
Regular Classroom Teacher	11.1%	7.7%
Vocational Education Teacher	33.3%	38.5%
Special Education Teacher	33.3%	30.8%
Multi-disciplinary Team	18.5%	11.5%

The curricular components of vocational programming were queried as
well. The responses reflected in Table 11.6 indicate that many of the same types

of curriculum components were emphasized at both junior and senior high school levels.

Table 11.6
Curriculum Components Included in Vocational Programs for Mildly Disabled Students

	Junior High			High School		
	Yes	No	No Response	Yes	No	No Response
Learning to Find a Job	55.6%	18.5%	25.9%	57.7%	3.8%	38.5%
Skills of Interviewing and Conversing	44.4%	22.2%	33.3%	50.0%	3.8%	46.2%
Learning to Fill Out Employment Forms	66.7%	11.1%	22.2%	57.7%	3.8%	46.2%
Learning to Use Money	66.7%	14.8%	18.5%	42.3%	15.4%	53.8%
Learning to Use Transportation Services	18.5%	44.4%	37.0%	30.8%	15.4%	53.8%
Acquiring Basic Skills Required for a Specific Job	40.1%	33.3%	25.9%	46.2%	11.5%	42.3%

In another area of inquiry, respondents at the high school level were asked if they bought or contracted services for vocational training of mildly handicapped students. It was evident that a large part of the training remained in-house. Results showed 3.8 percent of programs used vocational centers, no one was placed in community colleges, and 7.7 percent utilized external work study programs. Other vocational educational situations were used 4.8 percent of the time. The balance (83.7 percent) of the vocational training effort remained in the high schools.

Table 11.7
Curricular Components of Survival Academics in Vocational Programs for Mildly Handicapped Students

	Junior High			High School		
	Yes	No	No Response	Yes	No	No Response
Reading	70.4%	3.7%	25.9%	53.8%	3.8%	42.3%
Writing	70.4%	3.7%	25.9%	38.5%	11.5%	50.0%
Spelling	55.6%	7.4%	37.0%	42.3%	7.7%	50.0%
Math	70.4%	3.7%	25.9%	53.8%	3.8%	42.3%

Last, a question was asked to ascertain the curricular composition of survival academics included as part of vocational training efforts.

As the data in Table 11.7 indicate, there was a significantly greater number of affirmative statements for curricular components at the junior high school level when compared to the senior high level.

DOMAIN 4: INDIVIDUALIZED EDUCATION PLAN (IEP) SECTION

A series of questions were asked to assess how IEPs reflect vocational programming needs for mildly handicapped students at the secondary school level. When asked if IEPs include goals for specific vocational programming respondents from junior high settings indicated 29.6 percent yes, 59.3 percent no with 11.1 percent no response. Respondents from high school settings showed a higher affirmative response answering 42.3 percent yes, 53.8 percent no, and 3.8 percent no response.

In order to add specificity to the previous statement, a follow-up question was asked to determine if IEP goals were career awareness, prevocational or vocationally oriented. Junior high respondents indicated 25.9 percent career awareness, 44.4 percent prevocational, and 25.9 percent vocational goals. The

Table 11.8
Personnel Involved in the Development of
Vocationally Related Objectives on the IEP

		Yes	No	No Response
Parents	Junior High	48.1%	48.1%	3.7%
	High School	53.8%	26.9%	19.2%
Students	Junior High	44.4%	55.6%	0%
	High School	53.8%	26.9%	19.2%
Vocational/	Junior High	40.7%	59.3%	0%
Occupational	High School	30.8%	61.5%	7.7%
Education				
Teacher				
Special	Junior High	74.1%	7.4%	18.5%
Education	High School	57.7%	11.5%	30.8%
Teacher				

emphasis was somewhat different from high school respondents. They showed 38.5 percent career awareness, 38.5 percent prevocational, and 34.6 percent vocational goals.

Respondents also were queried to determine whether vocational objectives were based on vocational assessment data. Junior high teachers indicated 14.8 percent yes, 85.9 percent no, and 3.7 percent no response. High school teachers responded in a similar manner. They indicated 15.4 percent yes, 76.9 percent no with 7.7 percent no response.

Finally, questions were asked to determine the extent of involvement in the development of IEPs relative to vocational objectives. The role of students, parents, special educators and vocational educators was assessed.

As is shown in Table 11.8 at both the junior and senior high levels of instruction there was a significant amount of participation of students, parents, and special educators. Vocational educators showed a lesser degree of involvement.

DISCUSSION

Upon analyzing the data, it seems that there is an absence of a conceptual model for the vocational education of mildly handicapped students. Whereas the literature contains excellent theoretical program designs (Phelps 1977; Meers 1980) it is evident that there are problems with practical application. Parts of the vocational education puzzle are present, but they are simply not synthesized well.

The findings were disappointing in the areas of vocational assessment. Assessment for predictive purposes, placement decisions, individual educational programming and evaluation were markedly wanting. Whereas vocational assessment has been invaluable in the vocational programming of other exceptional populations, those who work with mildly handicapped students have not availed themselves of this methodology, and ultimately vocational prognosis cannot be based on reading level alone.

Symptomatic of the lack of a conceptual model is the extensive duplication at the junior and senior high school in career education, prevocational, and vocational training. Programs are not well articulated at these levels. Most significantly, there seems to be a lack of definitive sequencing of curricula that presupposes competency attainment for the next phase of vocational programming. The implications of developmental delay obviously interfere in the career/vocational education sequence (D'Alonzo 1977), but this does not happen to be the primary cause for the large overlap of curriculum.

It was very encouraging to find that at the junior and senior high levels there are vocational educational situations that simulate work environments. This has many positive implications for the transfer of skills from schools to vocational situations. Also it tends to close the gap of what goes on in school settings, and its practicality to what is going on in the the "real world."

Moreover, at the secondary school level the data show partnerships are being forged between special and vocational educational personnel. This is consistent with the emerging models of cooperation and interdisciplinary teamwork.

CONCLUSIONS

The results of this study clearly show that the fields of learning disabilities and career/vocational education are beginning to address the vocational needs of learning disabled and mildly handicapped individuals. The interface is not one that is easily accomplished however. Application of the generic principles of career/vocational education for these students is currently in a rudimentary state. Yet, the systems that are currently in place will serve students exceedingly well after they are fully developed and "fine-tuned." The key, however, will be a system that incorporates enough flexibility to address the divergent academic, social, and vocational needs of these students. This poses even greater challenges at the secondary school level.

While those who work with exceptional students rally around the concept of least restrictive environment at the secondary level, there must be an additional modifier to that concept. In working with learning disabled and mildly handicapped students, one must see secondary school efforts leading toward placement in the least restrictive vocational environment. This is described by Gerber (1982) as programming based on individual educational and vocational assessment data, underscored by alternatives and options in placement all along the career/vocational education continuum. It is culminated by a learning disabled or mildly handicapped individual who enters the job market with optimum use of acquired skills and working up to his or her maximum potential.

REFERENCES

D'Alonzo, B. "Trends and Issues in Career Education for the Mentally Retarded." *Education and Training of the Mentally Retarded* 12 (1977) 156-157.

Gerber, P. J. "Learning Disabilities and Vocational Education: Realities and Challenges." *Prevocational and vocational education for special needs youth,* edited by K.P. Lynch, W. E. Kiernan, and J. A. Stark. Baltimore, Md.: Paul H. Brookes Publishing Company, 1982. pp 185-198.

Meers, G. D. *Handbook of Special Vocational Needs Education.* Rockville, Md.: Aspen, 1980.

Mori, A. " Career Education for the Learning Disabled — Where are We Now?" *Learning Disabilities Quarterly* (1980) 3:91-101.

Phelps, L. A., and R.J. Lutz. *Career Exploration and Preparation for the Special Needs Learner.* Boston: Allyn and Bacon, 1977.

12

Survey of the Participants in the
Program of Assistance in Learning at
Curry College, Milton, Massachusetts, 1971–1980

Marijanet Doonan and Sheldon T. Boxer

In 1971, the Program of Assistance in Learning (PAL) at Curry College began in order to assist college-able, learning disabled students become self-learners functioning in a college environment. Since 1971, the program has grown to where it now has a waiting list, in addition to the seventy-plus students who are accepted as freshmen each year. Since the inception of the program in 1971, there has been no formal, objective, outside evaluation of the program, although informal evaluation has taken place during the years of operation. In order to become familiar with PAL, we became researchers with the program for a period of time extending over the years of 1978 through 1980. In addition to other research we collected, we wanted to learn more about PAL participants and their reactions to the program. Therefore, in 1980, we conducted a formal survey of the participants.

We had several reasons for undertaking this survey. First, we wanted to ascertain, in the eyes of former and current PAL students, if the program was meeting its objectives. Since no formal evaluation had occurred in regard to the program, the PAL staff supported this purpose. They wanted to know if their objectives were being met. These objectives were: to help the students learn to acquire meaningful information; to provide opportunities for the sharing of ideas; to develop communication skills; and to establish a sense of student self-worth.

Second, on the basis of our observations and interviews, we came to believe that much student growth and development occurred through participation in those components of PAL designed both to help students learn and to develop self-confidence. Therefore, through the questionnaire, we wanted to confirm or negate this assumption.

An additional reason for undertaking such a survey was to determine whether or not the process of gathering information through a questionnaire would be effective. Since little research had been done with this particular population, the results of the survey would provide interesting insight into the adult learning disabled population and its ability to serve as respondents in a more formal, structured approach to research.

PROCEDURE

To accomplish our purposes, we decided to use a mail questionnaire, even though there were two difficulties implicit in its use. First, there is a problem with the use of a survey for a learning disabled population that has difficulties in the decoding and encoding of written materials. Yet, because of the geographical diffusion of the population under study and the intervening time spans since their participation in PAL, our decision was that the written questionnaire was the only feasible approach. Furthermore, since this particular population had had special assistance in language skills, it was assumed that individuals might be especially motivated to try to answer the questionnaire — particularly since it was sent through PAL. Second, the survey instrument that was developed was ambitious in its attempt to obtain information, and its length may have limited the number of respondents completing the entire instrument. Yet, we decided to use the one longer questionnaire instead of two or more shorter ones because we felt that the same population might lose its motivation if more than one questionnaire were distributed.

In developing the questionnaire, we sought assistance from other pollsters, the PAL staff, and the college administration. We selected topics about which we wished to obtain information, developed questions, prepared the format for computer tabulation, and finally leveled the questions that were included to approximately a ninth-grade reading level.

The questionnaires were mailed in April 1980 to all those students who had participated in PAL since its inception in 1971; the names and addresses were provided by the PAL administration. Responses were voluntary. The respondents were asked to identify themselves on the survey instrument. A total of 131 questionnaires out of 320 questionnaires were completed and returned. A total of 31 participants could not be located either through PAL, Curry College, or the United States Postal Service after at least two attempts were made to locate each person. These questionnaires were returned unanswered. The rate of return of the questionnaires represents a 41 percent rate of return. To date, no additional follow-up has been used to increase the rate of return for this survey. However, a follow-up survey is planned for this year.

The information requested on the survey can be divided into four parts. Part I explores the educational history of the participants through high school with reference to their learning disability. Part II contains information about the relationship of the student participants to Curry College. Part III contains many of the important elements of the study since it involves the students' reactions to their association with PAL. Part IV includes the personal reactions of the participants to their family and personal life as related to learning disabilities. The results of the questionnaire resulted in hand coding of each response. These were then key-punched and run by computer using the Statistical Package for the Social Science (SPSS).

SUMMARY OF PART I — EDUCATIONAL HISTORY
OF THE PARTICIPANTS:
PRE-KINDERGARTEN THROUGH HIGH SCHOOL

In this section of the questionnaire, we wished to obtain background information about the identification of disabilities and the prior education of these students in order to get a historical perspective of their educational experiences. We were interested in knowing if there had been significant supportive assistance for these particular students and if this assistance had positively or negatively influenced their motivation or ability.

Of the 131 respondents, 40 percent had their language disability identified by parents; 3 percent identified their own learning disability; 39 percent were identified by teachers and school personnel; and 18 percent were identified by other sources which included family physicians and psychologists.

Since 39 percent were identified by school personnel, this result indicates a continuing need for awareness, sensitivity and training for school personnel in the identification of learning disabilities. In addition, it indicates the importance of parent awareness and the need for educated observations by parents and close communication between parents and schools.

Of the respondents with identified learning disabilities, 54 percent had these disabilities recognized before or during elementary school years, 39 percent had these disabilities recognized during junior high school or high school years, 7 percent of this population did not have their learning disability recognized until after high school.

Since early detection of learning disabilities has been considered important in providing essential supportive learning assistance and in preventing the development of feelings of inadequacy on the part of the students, these results are important. They indicate the need for increased observation, diagnosis, and identification at elementary levels.

Of the identified students, 50 percent had some form of remedial assistance throughout their school careers. In describing this assistance in the narrative section of the questionnaire, many students felt that the support services received had been inadequate although they did not cite specific reasons.

Based on the number of PAL participants who exhibit average to above-average intelligence as evidenced by the Wechsler Adult Intelligence Scale

(WAIS) testing, the student statements concerning the inadequacy of their prior learning assistance can be considered to have some legitimacy. Generally, for this controlled population, elementary and secondary schools did not seem to adequately meet the instructional needs of this learning disabled population who were academically able and capable of pursuing higher education. Although assistance had been given, it did not seem to provide sufficient instruction to support the type of learning independence needed in academic areas. In addition, if this population is to be considered typical, one of the by-products of the type of programming that was available to them in elementary and secondary schools seemed to develop, as an unfortunate side effect, a tremendous lack of self-confidence and lack of self-worth, as detailed in the narrative sections of the questionnaire.

In 35 percent of the cases, the students indicated that they probably would not have been able to function effectively in college without PAL assistance; 31 percent responded that they did not know if they could have handled college level work alone, adding that high school level work was extremely difficult for them. The historical perspective gained from the survey showed that parents and schools seem to share the equal burden of identification of the learning disabled and pressing for adequate support services. Over 54 percent of the students had early detection — before or during elementary school; yet 46 percent of the students were not identified at this early level and thus could not benefit from early intervention programs. Among the identified students, many did not receive any learning assistance that they now considered adequate, during their public school years. In addressing the question of the influences supportive assistance had on their motivation or ability, we relied on the written responses of the students in which 31 respondents indicated that they felt that this support had not been helpful and resented being taken out of class for special work.

SUMMARY OF PART II —
PARTICIPANTS' RELATIONSHIP TO CURRY COLLEGE

In this section, we wished to explore the respondents' reactions to Curry as a learning institution and to identify some of the factors that aid these students in developing motivation and self-concept.

Of the respondents, 35 percent were made aware of Curry's Program of Assistance in Learning through school personnel, administrators, teachers and guidance counselors; 29 percent learned of PAL through personal contacts outside their own educational institution; 18 percent learned of PAL through media publications; and 18 percent learned of Curry through other sources.

These statistics indicate several things. First, the importance of media in reporting successful programs and opportunities for non-traditional learners cannot be overlooked. Second, the need for increased programs in various fields with adequate support services for learning disabled people beyond the high school setting, and increased awareness, by the public, of these programs is a continuing need. Regular school personnel, parents, learning disabled students and special service school personnel need to keep increasing awareness of what is available. The results indicate that counseling programs at the junior high school and high school level for students with learning disabilities need to continuously update their information and to provide adequate information about post-high school programs for the learning disabled population who wish to continue education.

In the narrative portion of the survey, many respondents recounted years filled with major feelings of inadequacy when faced with academic tasks at elementary and junior high school levels. The survey was administered to all those who had participated in PAL for at least one year. Interestingly enough, once at Curry, 49 percent of the respondents felt that they were "about average" in comparison to the other students in ths college. Of those who answered the questionnaire, 29 percent rated themselves above average, and 18 percent rated themselves among the best students at Curry. Only 4 percent of the respondents indicated that they felt below average in comparison to other Curry students.

These responses seem to indicate that given the opportunity and supportive help, learning disabled students perform adequately in college settings and can recognize their own ability. The fact that these students feel good about themselves and their efforts is further indicated by responses in which 76 percent of the PAL population expressed satisfaction with Curry College and their relationship to it. In their rating of PAL students, more than 50 percent of the participants described their peers in PAL as studious, cooperative, friendly, and sympathetic. Less than 20 percent saw PAL students as lazy, uninformed or unfriendly. It is also interesting to note that only 2 percent of the students had indicated that their social contacts were limited to PAL students. In seeking relationships, 92 percent of the students had friends at Curry from the regular student body as well as from the PAL student group.

The PAL participants were asked in the survey to give information about how PAL students think other people view PAL. According to the respondents, 60 percent felt that non-PAL students at Curry did not react negatively to their PAL participation. Of these, 27 percent felt the reaction of other students to PAL participation was positive. Nineteen percent of the students were uncertain as to how others felt about their PAL participation.

In answering questions about the reaction of Curry to their PAL participation, the survey indicated that 44 percent of the professors viewed their PAL participation as positive; 46 percent indicated that they were either unsure of the reaction of the professors or they felt there was no reaction to report; only 5 percent of the respondents indicated that the professors viewed their participation as negative.

Since one of the objectives identified by PAL is that of enabling the participants to establish a sense of self-worth, the questionnaire responses in these areas can give us some information about this. PAL students felt that others viewed their participation in the program rather positively. This is somewhat unmeasurable, but is an important positive influence on the student's self-image. Also, it indirectly influences their motivation in a positive way. Thus, in looking at the respondents' positive reactions to Curry College, it is important to be aware of the influence this may have had in their success at PAL.

SUMMARY OF PART III —
RESPONDENTS' ASSOCIATION WITH PAL

In this section, we wanted to determine if PAL was meeting its objectives and what specific parts of the program, if any, actually supported this. Thus, in Part III, the questionnaire addressed areas relating to the Program of Assistance in Learning.

Among the resources available for PAL participants are: tape library of college texts; untimed examinations; subject area tutoring; spelling assistance; counseling in addition to specific programming for each student that includes five areas of skills development. These areas of skills development, in study skills, oral communication, writing, spatial relationships, and mathematics are the content areas of the PAL tutorials. The survey asked those who had participated in PAL to identify what specifically helped them acquire learning skills and develop independence.

For 85 percent of the students, PAL was at least an adequate place for them. For 95 percent of the respondents, the PAL staff was seen as having an interest in them as individuals. Eighty-one percent of the respondents indicated that they talked with the PAL staff outside of the instructional sessions. For 40 percent of these respondents, these discussions extended to subjects beyond strict academic areas. It is important to note, as a result of these responses, that the qualities needed in the instructional staff extend beyond those of proficiency in educational methodology and content. The responses, plus personal narratives in the questionnaires, indicate that students sought support, counseling, understanding and friendship from the staff. The students responded most favorably when asked to discuss the development of confidence gained through PAL. They referred to the constant encouragement they received from the PAL staff as being a major factor in helping them establish self-worth.

In addition to the results of this survey, our observations and discussions with PAL staff and administration caused us to stress the importance of the quality of interpersonal interactions with students. The concern, understanding and empathy of the staff may be a critical factor in the success of this particular program.

We also asked students to rate the importance of the various program components. The results indicate that aid in study techniques, untimed examinations, availability of instructors, and aid in written language were important to the students. Because not all students participated in all of the tutorial sessions, we cannot be sure, based on the results of this survey alone, that these results are truly reflective of the value of the components. It should be noted that the work in oral communications is a more recent addition to the program, and it may appear low in response only because fewer students had the opportunity to work through it. On the other hand, the students indicated that aid in mathematics and the opportunities for social relationships within the PAL setting were not very important to them.

Respondents were asked to identify the major program components that contributed to the development of independence in learning. The results indicate that the following were most helpful: PAL untimed exams; availability of tutorial sessions; availability of PAL instructors. In indicting those areas that were not helpful in developing independence, the respondents specified interaction with PAL students and the half-year support program. It is important to note that participation in the full year program is mandatory. The participation in the half-year support program that PAL provides for sophomores is recommended but voluntary, and not all respondents may have used it.

When asked to identify the components of PAL that could be improved, the students indicated that the content of the tutorials could use some improvement. For some students, the developmental approach is seen as boring. Yet, from observation, we have seen its necessity. The reactions of students in this response may reflect some sense of embarrassment they seem to feel with the elementary nature of the early tutorial sessions. In addition, there is an element of boredom and apprehension with the content since some of these areas have caused prior learning discomfort. Perhaps there is a way in which the staff could explain more fully the total ramifications of the process in each tutorial to the students and, thus, gain a more positive reaction.

Another area indicated by the students as needing some improvement is the awareness of the Curry College instructors of the students' participation in PAL. Interestingly, according to the staff, the students bear the responsibility for notifying their instructors. This is voluntary and is done only by the student. Once again, this may reflect a sense of hesitancy and discomfort felt by the PAL participants about their learning disabilities even with others who can help them. Perhaps, here again, the PAL staff could take the initiative and be more them. Perhaps, here again, the PAL staff could take the initiative and be more aware of this reluctance when it occurs and take steps to assist.

To summarize the results of this section, we must remind the reader that our primary objective was to determine if the objectives of PAL were being met by the type of assistance the program provided. The first objective of Curry's Program of Assistance in Learning is to assist students to learn how to acquire meaningful information. The second is to help students comprehend the information and synthesize it. We can look to several indicators to determine if these are met.

Many students were able to maintain a sufficiently adequate grade point average to remain at Curry for the second semester of their freshman year. This is a possible indicator of their ability to acquire and synthesize information.

If we accept the premise that college presents meaningful information and requires students to conceptualize it, then we can look again to the survey for indicators of success in Curry's Program of Assistance in Learning as it attempts to meet these first two goals. Students were asked to indicate the number of college credits they had earned. The ability of 39 percent of the respondents to complete more than 120 college credits allows us to conclude that Curry meets its objectives of helping students in the acquisition of meaningful information and the successful comprehension and synthesis of this information. Since 32 percent of the participants are still in college, this percentage can be expected to increase.

The third objective of PAL is to provide students with the opportunity to share ideas and develop communication skills. The survey questions designed to assess the specific content components of PAL asked for specific reactions to those involving written language and oral communication. Response from students indicated that these were areas of major assistance. Written language was considered important by 82 percent of the respondents, while oral communication was considered important by 59 percent. From our observations at Curry over two years, we noticed that some students were not aware of their difficulties in oral communication; they were unaware of what oral communication encompasses and how it facilitates learning and human interaction. An additional factor should be noted here: oral communication is a component that was introduced in 1978-79, and many of the respondents may not have worked through the tutorial. For this reason, this particular finding will be reviewed again next year, once this component is more firmly established.

The ability of students to respond adequately in the narrative section of the questionnaire can be considered an indicator of the achievement of the PAL goals in developing communication and sharing ideas. Their ability to respond to the questionnaire gives a measure of information about the quality of the students' handling of encoding and decoding somewhat difficult written material. From the narratives written by some of the respondents, additional information can be gleaned. When commenting on the components, students stated:

> Untimed exams greatly helped. This lessened the pressure.

> PAL gave me a place to go to talk to someone about problems. They listened.

> PAL has helped me to improve some of the specific problems that have been
> bothering me about school, such as grammar, reading, and study habits.

SUMMARY OF PART IV — PERSONAL BACKGROUND
OF THE RESPONDENTS AND THEIR REACTIONS
TO LEARNING DISABILITIES

In this section, we wished to find out what relationship learning disabilities had
to the students' sense of self-worth as individuals, since the fourth objective of
the Program of Assistance in Learning was to develop a sense of self-worth in
the students. In Part IV of the survey, students provided personal reflections
about being learning disabled and its effect on their family, social, emotional,
educational and professional lives. Out of the 131 respondents, there were 105
instances of learning disability in the family. It is interesting to note that the
results of our sampling correspond to the findings of other studies in relationship to the higher rate of incidence of learning disability among the male population (Kirk and Gallagher 1979; Kranes 1980; Meier 1971). In our sampling,
47 percent of the respondents had a history of family instances of learning
disabilities in related males, while 17 percent had this history in related females. If further study continues to support male dominance in identified instances of learning disabilities, this could explain, in part, one of the reasons
more male students tend to be found in special education settings. These findings neither confirm nor deny heredity as a causal factor in learning disabilities,
but it provides suggestions for additional research.

For 48 percent of the students, being learning disabled had some effect
on their social life. In the written narrative sections, some students expanded
on this. One student noted difficulty with old friends because of placement
in a special educational residential school at the age of ten. Another student
indicated that there was a need to constantly make excuses about inability
to read street signs by stating that glasses had been forgotten. A third student mentioned total unawareness of non-verbal signals sent by people in regular conversation, causing extensive difficulty, especially in male/female
relationships.

One interesting note is that 37 percent of the students felt that certain occupations were not possible for them to pursue because they were learning disabled. Some of these were: medicine; politics; flight industries; secretarial areas; science-related industries; and those areas requiring writing, such as journalism.

The narratives generally reflected advice to those who work with the learning disabled. One of the most often cited areas for comment was that learning disabled students need encouragement and recognition. These students said:

> Like myself, I'm sure many of these students were never even recognized in school because we were so quiet. Just being recognized means a lot.

> Make sure students know that being learning disabled is not the end of the world. Honesty is important. Make sure that the students know that learning disabilities can't be eliminated but the effects can be neutralized and programs like PAL can help to do this.

In addition, the respondents indicated that PAL provided support for them as students and as individuals. This can be illustrated by citing some of their comments:

> PAL opened up many doors for me. It allowed me the chance to see that I could be very successful academically.

> PAL has helped me to understand where I need to get my act together.

> PAL made me feel I am as good as anyone else. It helped to get me back on the road again.

The reactions of 81 percent of the respondents have been positive to their PAL experience. In addition, the narratives give specific support to the personal self-worth now felt by the students. Some of them have written:

> The program helped me accept myself, to function successfully in college and to feel worthy of other friendships.

> I was very fortunate to enter the PAL program. Someone was always there to listen and to truly make me feel that I was a beautiful and intelligent person.

One of the major keys to sucess is the development of personal self-worth. Certainly, this program seems to develop this in those who participate.

With newly developed confidence resulting from carefully structured programming that leads to success and achievement, students seem able to function adequately and successfully. As one student so aptly wrote:

> PAL gave me the confidence to think that I could achieve; that I could go to college; that I could go and do the work. The staff was super. They supported and guided me, but made me work. Without PAL, I would not be a college graduate today.

CONCLUSIONS

For the 41 percent of the respondents to this questionnaire, PAL was helpful to them in reestablishing their rights and abilities to pursue meaningful education beyond the secondary level. That PAL has been able to document this kind of success with 131 of its students out of a total of 320 is notable. However, because these responses may over-represent those students who benefitted most from the program, we are planning to conduct another study to gather additional information from a random selection of former PAL students who did not respond to the written questionnaire. Perhaps, some of them benefitted as much from the program as those who responded, but had trouble with the long questionnaire, or, perhaps, others were unable to perform academically as they had hoped and did not want to work through the questionnaire for it confronted them, once again, with their problems in reading and responding appropriately. Information from the students who did not respond to our questionnaire is needed to supplement these initial findings, thus a follow-up study is planned by the authors.

REFERENCES

Kirk, S. A., and J. J. Gallagher. *Educating Exceptional Children.* Boston: Houghton Mifflin, 1972.

Kranes, J. E. *The Hidden Handicap.* New York: Simon and Schuster, 1980.

Meier, J. "Prevalence and Characteristics of Learning Disabilities Found in Second Grade Children." *Journal of Learning Disabilities,* (1971): 6-19.

Nie, N., C. H. Hull, J. Jenkins, K. Steinbrenner, B. Bent. *Statistical Package for the Social Sciences.* New York: McGraw-Hill, 1975.

Wechsler, David. *WAIS Manual — Wechsler Adult Intelligence Scale.* New York: The Psychological Corporation, 1955.

EARLY EDUCATION AND
ACTIVITY PROGRAMS

13

Using the Chicago EARLY Program to Catch and Correct Learning Disabilities at a Preschool Level

Nancy K. Naron and Anne Y. Campbell

Oᴜʀ ᴄᴏɴᴄᴇʀɴ concern in Chicago has been to direct efforts toward catching and correcting learning problems *before* the children encounter school failure. Current research does in fact indicate that all children can learn when instruction is appropriate to their needs (Bloom 1976), and that the earlier intervention is provided, the more likely children will be successful in school (Lazar et al. 1977). As a result of such findings on the importance of early childhood education as well as current legislation regarding the rights of the handicapped (PL 94-142), the necessity to identify young children's special needs and to provide appropriate instruction at the prekindergarten level is becoming widely accepted. The Chicago EARLY Program (*E*arly *A*ssessment and *R*emediation *L*aborator*Y*) was carefully developed over a five-year period to meet this need. Its materials, which are owned by The Chicago Board of Education, are nationally distributed by Educational Teaching Aids, 159 West Kinzie Street, Chicago, Illinois 60610.

TARGET POPULATION

The goal of the Chicago EARLY Program is to identify and provide remediation for children at a prekindergarten age who are likely to have later school learning problems. In particular, EARLY is designed to help identify that type of child who has normal intelligence, but who demonstrates a large discrepancy between abilities in different skill areas. Such a child is clearly more difficult to identify at an early age than a child with a more severe or obvious handicap, such as mental retardation, deafness, or a crippling disease. Children with more obvious exceptionalities are usually spotted by parents or pediatricians while the child is still quite young. Children with learning difficulties, on the other hand, are most often not identified until they are well into their school years (Naron 1981) and have already experienced the feelings of frustration and inadequacy associated with failure.

TARGET SKILLS

Because our task is to identify and help pre-reading and pre-writing children who are likely to have difficulty learning those skills, we operationalized the skills at a preschool level by means of a simplified information-processing model (Naron 1977). This model analyzes three important components of the precursor skills to reading and writing: *input* or how the child receives the information (auditorily or visually), *output* or how the child responds to indicate understanding (by a verbal or by a motor response), and *processing* or how the child processes the information from input to output (on a rotely learned or on a conceptual basis). Information about these three components provides a framework within which to identify a child's strengths and weaknesses as well as to develop appropriate remedial prescriptions.

DESCRIPTION OF THE EARLY MATERIALS

EARLY consists of two major components: an identification component and a remediation component. Detailed descriptions of the development, field-testing, and validation of the EARLY materials have been presented elsewhere (Naron 1977; Naron 1978; Naron, Katz, Murray, Rivera, and Washington 1979; Naron and Perlman 1981; and Perlman, Naron, Hiestand, and Sarther 1981). The section below will highlight the key points of the developmental process and will describe the materials as they appear in final form.

Identification

The Chicago EARLY Assessment is a short, individually administered screening test (with instructions in English and Spanish) that was carefully developed, field-tested, and validated over a period of several years. The 23 items on the assessment yield a score in each of five skill areas: gross motor, fine motor, visual discrimination, language, and memory. The items were selected on the basis of six general sources:
1. the potentially predictive elements set out in the EARLY information-processing model;
2. characteristics of school-age learning disabled children (Lerner 1971);
3. developmental milestones expected to be passed by the average child of this age, e.g., Goldman and Martin (1971);
4. the results of longitudinal research aimed at prediction questions, e.g., Stevenson et al. (1976);

5. the framework of already existing preschool screening and diagnostic devices, e.g., the Denver Developmental Screening Test by Frankenburg et al. (1967); and

6. the results of a pilot study conducted in Chicago to determine the most appropriate level of difficulty of items for youngsters in a large urban area.

Norming

The Chicago EARLY Assessment was normed on approximately 2,000 Chicago children between the ages of 3 and 5 years. The norming sample is representative of any large urban area such as Chicago, with approximately 54 percent of the children being black, 30 percent white, 11 percent Hispanic, and 5 percent other. Both sexes are equally represented, and the sample includes children who had preschool experience as well as those who did not. The norming sample is also characterized by a broad range of parental income and occupational status.

Concurrent validity

A comprehensive study (Naron 1977) was conducted to determine how closely a child's performance on the EARLY Assessment would match the results of a full diagnostic evaluation. A large number of diagnostic measures were selected to measure the same skills as measured by the assessment. Based upon teacher ratings, a group of 140 preschool-age children were selected to participate in the validation study. Half of these children were rated as likely to have school learning problems, and half were rated as not likely to have problems. All of the children were administered the EARLY Assessment, a hearing and vision test, and the approximately three hours of diagnostic measures. All the parents completed a parent questionnaire as well.

Based on the results of the diagnostic evaluation, the professional staff made decisions as to which children indicated potential problems later in school and which children were not likely to have learning problems. The decisions were based on two types of evidence: (1) the mental age of the child, as determined by the Leiter International Performance Scale (Leiter 1969) and (2) the profile of diagnostic test scores for each child. This conceptualization is an extension of the definition of a learning disabled child as one who has average or above average intelligence but is achieving at a much lower level than he/she is capable (Lerner 1971). The score on the Leiter was considered an indicator of expected achievement; the scores on the diagnostic measures were considered an indicator of actual achievement. A profile was considered a learning disability profile when a large discrepancy was present between the child's performance on the visual-motor tasks and his or her performance on the auditory-verbal tasks.

Although the study analyzed several types of classifications, this discussion will focus on the two most relevant: those children not likely to have school learning problems, and those who had normal intelligence and a learning disability profile of test scores. (The classifications were used for research purposes only. Information imparted to teachers and parents was in terms of each child's strengths and weaknesses.)

Three major analyses were conducted to determine the most accurate and cost-effective means of identifying the children with potential learning disabilities. The diagnostic classifications were entered into a discriminant analysis with the three following variables individually: (1)the items on the EARLY Assessment, (2) the items on the parent questionnaire, and (3) the teacher ratings. The purpose of these analyses was to discover how well each of these "short-cut" variables could predict what three hours of diagnostic testing would predict.

The results of these analyses are summarized below:

1. The 15-20 minute EARLY Assessment accurately discriminated the children with potential learning disabilities in more than 90 percent of the cases.

2. The parent questionnaire accurately discriminated the children with potential learning disabilities in only 75 percent of the cases. When the parent information was used in conjunction with the EARLY Assessment, the accuracy was no higher than with the EARLY variable alone.

3. Although the teachers were quite accurate in identifying the children with no problems and the children with low mental age, the ratings by the prekindergarten teachers were quite inadequate for identifying the potentially learning disabled children. Specifically, the teachers rated as not likely to have problems 67 percent of the children who were pinpointed by the diagnostic evaluation as potentially learning disabled. This is not surprising, considering these children have normal intelligence and are not yet in a sutiation where an information-processing deficit would be obvious (Naron 1981).

Predictive validity

More recently, an initial longitudinal study (Perlman et al. 1981) has been conducted with about 650 children to determine the actual predictive ability of the EARLY Assessment. Some definite relationships were found between performance on the EARLY Assessment and school learning problems three to five years later. The relationships vary by the age of the child at time of testing and the specific measures of later performance. The variable of learning and psychomotor difficulties in the classroom, as measured by a follow-up teacher questionnaire, appears to be most consistently related to the results of the EARLY Assessment. This is the criterion variable which is closest to measuring what the EARLY Assessment purports to measure. Therefore, the EARLY Assessment definitely has some validity in predicting later school learning problems. However, since many learning problems do not show up until much later than the second grade, continued follow-up of these children beyond the primary grades will be necessary to obtain more complete information.

Reliability

Test reliability refers to the consistency and stability of evaluation results. The EARLY Assessment has been found to have very good reliability (Perlman et al. 1981), with a coefficient alpha of .89 for the total test (standardized item alpha = .93). Test-retest reliability examined over a one-week interval resulted in coefficients ranging from .72 to .91 for the five subscales. Interrater reliability coefficients for the five subscales were found to range from .87 to .98, and indicate that classroom teachers give the assessment as reliably as trained outside testers do.

Remediation

As soon as the evidence indicated that potentially learning disabled prekindergarten children could be identified with reasonable accuracy and cost-effectiveness, we turned our efforts toward the development of an intervention program for such children. We felt strongly that it is pointless (and possibly harmful) to diagnose problems which cannot or will not be directly remediated, and we therefore gave as much careful attention to this component as to that of identification.

The *Chicago EARLY Instructional Activities for Ages 3-5* is the final product of a great deal of pilot work conducted with prekindergarten children identified as having potential learning problems. These materials are based on the same information-processing model as the screening procedure, and are specifically aimed at remediating each child's particular deficit area (visual-motor, auditory-verbal). Because the target children are not severely handicapped, but rather have particular cognitive needs, the program is conceived as supplementary to other early childhood programs.

The intervention program is based on sequential, developmental objectives in three main skill areas: Body Image/Gross Motor, Perceptual-Motor (including arithmetic), and Language. The area of Body Image/Gross Motor incorporates both motor and language activities and is viewed as preliminary to both the Perceptual-Motor and Language curricula. The Perceptual-Motor activities teach fine motor and visual discrimination skills. They incorporate the content areas of color, shape, size, familiar objects, and arithmetic — and proceed from basic discrimination (matching) skills to higher-level conceptual skills (e.g., recall of what is missing). The Language activities are aimed at increasing communication skills, and emphasize both receptive language (i.e., comprehension) and expressive language (i.e., speaking). These activities proceed from basic auditory discrimination skills through simple sentence-building, to reasoning and interpretive thinking skills. Activities geared toward improving a child's memory, both auditory and visual, are found throughout the curriculum.

The sequential (developmental) approach upon which the program is based derives from the notion that earlier, simpler skills build the foundation for those that are more complex. Using such an ordered list of skills gives the teacher a great deal of flexibility and control. In the program, the EARLY Assessment is linked directly to the curriculum. For each assessment item that a child may fail, the teacher is directed to the appropriate curriculum area and objective. As a result, the teacher can pinpoint where in the skill-list a child's ability is inadequate and can begin teaching at that point. If that level is too difficult for the child, the teacher can move backward in the list of objectives until the child's present level of success is ascertained.

A small experimental pilot program (Naron et al. 1979) was conducted to determine the efficacy of providing prekindergarten children with structured, individualized instruction to supplement their regular preschool experiences. Thirty-two children were selected to participate based upon test profiles (such as those used in the validation study) indicating potential learning difficulties. Each child received instruction on the curriculum area in which he/she indicated a weakness for one hour a day, four days a week, for three months. Parent participation in the program was heavily encouraged.

Pre- and post-tests designed to measure skills in the visual-motor and the auditory-verbal areas were administered to the target children and to a comparison group who had exhibited similar profiles but for one reason or another had been unable to enroll in the pilot program. Significant gains were found for the EARLY children in both skill areas, with the children who received remediation in a given skill area scoring even higher than the whole group in that particular skill area. Furthermore, those children whose parents participated in the program indicated tremendous gains on the auditory-verbal tests. Such gains indicate the extra impact that is possible when concerned parents are given specific appropriate suggestions for home interactions with their children.

USE OF THE EARLY MATERIALS
IN THE CHICAGO PUBLIC SCHOOLS

The Chicago public schools provide educational services for approximately 11,000 prekindergarten-age children each year. Of these, about 10,000 are enrolled in regular prekindergarten programs while about 1,000 are enrolled in special education prekindergarten. The EARLY materials are used flexibly in the different programs according to the specific needs of the participating children.

Regular Prekindergarten

Regular Chicago prekindergarten classrooms generally fall into two categories: Head Start and Title I Early Childhood Programs (e.g., child-parent centers). The EARLY materials are an integral part of these early childhood programs. In the fall of each year, all entering prekindergarteners are administered the Chicago EARLY Assessment by the classroom teacher. After testing, the teacher uses conversion tables in the assessment manual to translate each child's five skill area scores into equivalent percentile ranks according to the child's age level. The teacher then plots the scores on a classroom summary sheet that is designed to: (1) pinpoint each child's specific deficits (e.g., colors) as well as any general areas of need (e.g., visual discrimination), and (2) group the children for instruction according to their identified needs. The teacher is given guidelines on how to relate this test information to the instructional activities component, as well as guidelines for when to retest and/or refer a child for further evaluation.

After the first year of full citywide implementation of the EARLY materials in the regular Chicago public prekindergarten programs (the 1979-80 school year), a comprehensive teacher questionnaire was administered to determine the teachers' evaluation of the materials. A detailed account of the results of this questionnaire is presented elsewhere (Naron & Perlman, 1981). Generally, the 176 teacher respondents were overwhelmingly favorable in their reaction to the program, placing particular emphasis on the practicality and usefulness of the materials. Overall, the teachers indicated that using the EARLY materials helped them to do their job better.

Special Education Prekindergarten

The Chicago public schools have a strong commitment to provide services not only to the "normal" prekindergarten child, but also to meet the needs of children requiring special/exceptional services. These services fall into two main categories: those for children who are not presently attending any Chicago public prekindergarten program, and those for children who are placed in special education preschool classrooms.

Non-attending children

Federal, state, and local guidelines require than an active "child find" process be maintained by the school system for identifying prekindergarten-age children with special needs. For children who do not presently attend a Chicago public prekindergarten program, a referral for a comprehensive case study may originate from any of a number of sources: parents, health facilities (e.g., clinics, hospitals, private doctors), private preschools, or day care centers. Before special education placement and programming can be determined, the child must be given an indepth assessment. Children are referred to an Educational Diagnostic Center (EDC) where a team of specialists conducts a comprehensive case study to determine the need and degree of services to be provided. The role of the educational diagnostician is synonymous with that of the classroom teacher: to provide information related to the child's educational level and needs.

The Chicago EARLY Assessment gives the educational diagnostician an immediate and comprehensive glimpse of the child's abilities in the cognitive and motor domains. Since the items on the assessment tap the child's ability to encode, process, and use information through both the visual and auditory modalities, the diagnostician is able to quickly pinpoint the child's strengths and weaknesses. Depending on the nature and severity of the child's involvement, the diagnostician uses the assessment in a flexible manner. Children whose behavior and/or involvement make it impossible for them to tolerate indepth testing are usually able to attend to the task requirements of the EARLY Assessment. The diagnostician couples the results of the assessment with observations and parental input to form an educational diagnostic evaluation.

The educational diagnostician joins the other members of the staffing team to determine appropriate educational placement for each child. Appropriate placement is determined by the results of the comprehensive case study evaluation which includes but is not necessarily limited to an indepth: (1) educational, (2) speech and language, (3) social, (4) medical, and (5) psychological evaluation.

The staffing team may choose from three placement/programming options for a prekindergarten child: (1) a regular classroom with any needed remediation provided by the regular classroom teacher, (2) regular placement with specific services provided by a special education teacher (dual enrollment), and (3) self-contained special education placement. An individual educational program (IEP) is developed for each child who is programmed to receive special education services of any degree. The design of the Chicago EARLY Instructional Activities serves as an immediate guide to the establishment and management of the IEP objectives. By linking the child's performance on the EARLY Assessment to the correlated objectives of the curriculum, the diagnostician helps to develop an IEP that is suitable for that child and is educationally sound.

Attending children

Once the staffing team determines that a prekindergarten-age child is in need of special education services, that child is enrolled in an Early Childhood Education of the Handicapped (ECEH) classroom. The ECEH classroom setting is of a prescriptive-diagnostic nature where ongoing assessment and diagnostic services are provided as a means of continually meeting the needs of each child. Federal, state, and local guidelines do not permit the labeling of prekindergarten children with specific handicapping conditions; however, the symptomology exhibited is characteristic of children in categorized special education programs. Not unlike most preschool settings, parental involvement is a vital component of this program, with coordination of an effective school-home program deemed essential for the child's desired progress to be established and maintained.

The goals of the ECEH program are (1) to meet the individual educational needs of each child through the use of developmental guidelines, (2) to provide experiences that will develop each child's positive self-concept by allowing him/her to freely explore the environment cognitively, socially, and affectively, and (3) to establish an atmosphere that stimulates a desire to learn in each child. The use of the Chicago EARLY materials facilitates the meeting of these goals by insuring that each child is receiving instruction appropriate to his or her level and needs.

SUMMARY

The educational implications of the successful use of the Chicago EARLY materials in a wide variety of settings are far-reaching. By all indications, it is possible not only to identify children with potential learning problems at an early age, but also to ameliorate such problems while the children are still quite young. The benefits which can be derived from such early assessment and remediation are two-fold. One benefit is to the school system, which will profit by the reduction in the number of children who will need special education services during their later school years. The most important benefit is to the individual child, who rather than meeting the feelings of frustration and inadequacy typically associated with failure, will instead meet the feelings of success and self-esteem that are so important to a productive school career.

REFERENCES

Bloom, B. S. *Human Characteristics and School Learning*. New York: McGraw-Hill, 1976.

Frankenburg, W. K., J. Dodds, and A. Fandel. *Denver Developmental Screening Test*. Denver: University of Colorado Medical Center, 1967.

Goldman, J., and R. Martin. "Developmental Sequences: Steps in the Development of the Child from Birth through Five." Paper compiled at the request of the Governor's Committee on Special Learning. University of Wisconsin, 1971.

Lazar, I., V. Hubbell, H. Murray, M. Rosche, and J. Royce. *The Persistence of Preschool Effects* (Report No. 18-76-07843). Washington, D.C.: The Administration on Children, Youth, and Families, Office of Human Development Services, U.S. Dept. of Health, Education, and Welfare, September 1977.

Leiter, R. *The Leiter International Performance Scale*. Chicago: Stoelting, 1969.

Lerner, J. *Children with Learning Disabilities*. Boston: Houghton Mifflin, 1971.

Naron, N. K. "A realistic approach to the problem of early assessment and remediation of school learning problems in a large urban setting" (ERIC, ED 152 818). Paper presented at the meeting of the American Educational Research Association, New York City, April 1977.

———. "A tested approach to the prediction and treatment of learning disabilities at a preschool level." Paper presented at the Second National Invitational Conference on Communication Research in M.R. and L.D., Monmouth, Oregon, November 1978.

———. "The Big Cover-up." *Early Years*, March 1981.

Naron, N. K., N. Katz, C. G. Murray, C. D. Rivera, and T. Washington. "The prevention of learning disabilities before school: Results of a pilot program" (ERIC, ED 170 989). Paper presented at the meeting of the American Educational Research Association, San Francisco, April 1979.

Naron, N. K., and C. L. Perlman. "Chicago EARLY Program: Initial implementation of a preventative prekindergarten program" (ERIC, ED 201 382). Paper pre-

Angeles, April 1981.

Perlman, C. L., N. K. Naron, N. Hiestand, and C. Sarther. "Chicago EARLY Program follow-up: A longitudinal analysis" (ERIC, ED 204 372). Paper presented at the annual meeting of the American Educational Research Association, Los Angeles, April 1981.

Stevenson, H., T. Parker, A. Wilkinson, A. Hegion, and E. Fish. "A longitudinal study of individual differences in cognitive development and scholastic achievement." *Journal of Educational Psychology* 68, no. 4, (1976): 377-400.

14

The Use of Play in the Curriculum as a Vehicle for Diagnostic Assessment of the Young Learning Disabled Child

Gayle Mindes

WHAT IS PLAY?

PLAY IS an elusive construct to define. A variety of definitions have been advanced, each reflecting the broader conceptual framework of the individual author. There is no widespread, universal definition (Berlyne 1968; Ellis 1973; Neumann 1971) from the perspective of the function of play in the development of children. So viewed, play can be defined as a complex process, involving social, cognitive, physical and emotional elements, of relating to an aspect of reality as not serious or real. For the child this characterization makes it possible to relate to things that might otherwise be confusing, frightening, mysterious, irrelevant, risky, or forbidden. In this manner the child evolves competencies and defenses. The process has a developmental sequence. This definition draws support from those definitions concerned with play as a dynamic process. Theories which represent this point of view have been advanced by the following: Erikson (1963); Issacs (1933); Millar (1968); Piaget (1962); Valentine (1938); White (1959). From this theoretical position play can be described as sustained, absorbing, active, purposeful, joyful; an opportunity for practice of new skills and for discovery of the child's world. In an anthropological review, Bruner describes play as a "means of minimizing the consequences of one's actions and of learning, therefore in a less risky situation . . . (an) opportunity to try combinations of behavior that would, under functional pressures never be tried" (Bruner 1972, p. 693).

WHAT ROLE DOES PLAY SERVE IN THE CHILD'S DEVELOPMENT?

Play functions as a vehicle for growth of the child. In an interaction and exploration of his or her environment, the child gradually develops increasing competencies as an independent individual. The growth through play can be observed in the changing character of children's play at different ages. Identifiable stages of play have been described by Erikson (1963), Freud (1965), Peller (1954), Piaget (1962). The play of the child at a given age reflects the primary developmental issues of the period. Thus infant play is observed as centered around the body. The infant's attention is focused on the sound, smells, and sights around. The infant is tirelessly eager, repetitive. The infant plays Peek-a-Boo with mother, tries making all kinds of sounds, and gradually broadens his or her horizon as he or she begins crawling and walking further.

Toddler play extends to the world of small toys (Erikson 1963). The toddler takes delight in getting in and out of boxes and baskets, dropping and carrying objects, splashing water. At this age the young child becomes interested in fine motor sensory discrimination and motor coordination activities as well. The child begins to try buttons, zippers, puzzles, and crayons. Climbing, running, and other large muscle activities still excite the young toddler, who has ever increasing competency in these activities. Word play is another feature of toddler play: "No, no, no" in a very loud voice, accompanied by finger shaking perhaps; favorite nursery rhymes, "All the king's horses, all the king's horses"; repetition of words as a prompt to the adult, Child: "Woof, woof," Adult: "Are you a dog?", Child: "I not a dog."

Language and action gain increasing sophistication as the young child grows. Preschoolers begin to symbolically represent their world in dramatic play. At this stage young children play out familiar and unfamiliar, real and imagined themes: grocery store, baby, mother, school, Superman, Hulk, etc. In this play the child has an opportunity to try roles and develop a sense of self. Preschool children have greater ability to construct representation of their world with blocks, clay, paint, and crayons. They can represent absent objects through make believe. Preschoolers have the capacity to use materials more systematically and can interact with peers cooperatively and creatively. Simple games become a feature of the play of the older preschool child: Ring-around-the-Rosie; London Bridge is Falling Down. The complexity of games increases and overt fantasy play decreases as the young child grows to school age. Games with rules continue as a feature of the play of older children and adults (Erikson 1963; Piaget 1962).

WHAT ARE SOME ASSUMPTIONS ABOUT THE DEVELOPMENT OF YOUNG LEARNING DISABLED CHILDREN?

Handicap, within a broad range, is defined by the specific culture and social setting (Goffman 1963; Hobbs 1975; Morse 1979). This being the case, are learning disabled children sufficiently similar to non-disabled children? The assumption of similar developmental pattern has been variously tested in a variety of empirical studies for each of the traditional handicapping conditions (Gallagher 1975).

The developmental profiles of "learning disabled children" — as described by theory, case study, and empirical study — reflect developmental deviations primarily in the cognitive area. These cognitive deviations are described as occurring in sensory-motor: visual and auditory; perceptual-motor: body image and spatial relations; language: oral and written; and information processing (Farnham-Diggory 1978; Lerner 1976; Johnson and Myklebust 1967). In addition, Johnson and Myklebust (1967) describe a type of learning disability "as a disturbance in social perception. This aspect of behavior may be defined as the ability to immediately identify and recognize the meaning and significance of the behavior of others" (1967, 34). Recent research (Bryan 1981) has focused more attention toward the social perceptual problems of the learning disabled which may occur on a more generalized basis and thus influence child play patterns.

An additional factor affecting the learning disabled child's development is the child's family relationships. The emotional impact of a child with learning disabilities on his family is described as a disorganizing and emotionally upsetting factor, equivalent in distress impact to that of a physical disability (Farnham-Diggory 1978). To the extent that an individual child's family is able to cope with the crisis and upset, the impact of emotional/social problems for the child may be somewhat minimized. As Mogford (1977) puts it, "all handicapped children have one thing in common — that their ability to explore, interact with and master the environment is impaired, with a consequent distortion or deprivation of normal childhood experience" (p. 171).

In summary, the development of learning disabled children can be described as following the development trends of normal development with specific deviations based on the nature of the learning disability, the child's perception of his capacity and worth as an individual, as well as the response of the social world to the child.

FREE PLAY IN THE CURRICULUM FOR
THE PRESCHOOL LEARNING DISABLED CHILD

In a free play situation, the young learning disabled child can practice and master many skills and concepts. For the purposes of discussion, free play is defined as a substantive portion of a group classroom experience which is set aside for child-initiated play and exploration of developmentally appropriate materials and activities (30 to 45 minutes). The teacher's role in this situation is that of facilitator. This role begins with a careful choice of appropriate materials and classroom design which will start at the developmental level of the young learning disabled child and provide appropriate challenge. Additionally, the teacher must be prepared to advance play themes. As described above, the young child with learning disabilities may exhibit an atypical developmental pattern in play situations, depending on his particular disorder and his self-perception as well as various group issues arising from the particular group interrelationships or classroom dynamics.

In the free play situation the young disabled child can develop a sense of competence as he plays. The play process is both cognitive and affective, an interaction of the states; for example, cognitive problem solving can lead to increased social understanding. Play also incorporates opportunities for the development of motor coordination and perception, both fine and gross motor.

Examples of how the typical child begins to obtain mastery of demands placed upon him in school situations are as follows:

Conforming to routines:	In play the child may develop ritualistic activities that are representative of the routines established at home and at school. As a part of this play, the child may develop and enforce rules, both in a remembered and exaggerated form — "I'll beat you, if you don't eat your dinner."
Independence:	"Watch me, I can do it." Children building with blocks, determining how a meal should be served, outwardly express feelings of mastery.
Cooperation:	"It's my turn now." "You can't have it, it's mine." Through the resolution of such conflicts, initially with adult help, the child can moderate disputes for himself or play out imaginary disputes and sharing experiences.
Impulse control:	By playing out resistances to temptation — "The cat ate the cake, I didn't," and excesses of emotion — "Ow, ow, ow, he's killing me," the child practices limit setting and conformance, as well as different styles of moderating his impulses.
Communication:	More advanced play in groups requires verbal elaboration; often, therefore, the child learns

Competition skills:	At this age level, the development of these skills begins to increase through an assurance and confidence in self. Play allows the child the opportunity to repeat and practice, to try out new combinations, in order to foster the development of this foundation of competition, which typically is fostered in schools at ages five and six.
Assume responsibility:	Playing of the caring roles observed and sharing roles required, allows the child opportunity to develop skills.
Appropriate affect:	Playing out the matching of crying, laughing, and despair with the appropriate bodily gestures and language facilitates the development of appropriate affect.
Frustration:	Playing out themes, building with blocks demands a successive approximation of desired ends. This trial and error experience prepares the child for the real world of academic tasks.

The demands made on the young child with learning disabilities include conformance to the structure of classroom routines, maintenance of some measures of independence, cooperative behavior with peers and teachers, impulse control, effective communication with peers and teachers, assumption of responsibility as a group member, maintenance of appropriate affect and frustration tolerance for new academic tasks. If these social and emotional aspects of the child's functioning are too deviant, he cannot function cognitively and usually cannot match himself appropriately in the usual large group setting.

All of these skills can be developed and enhanced through play. As the young learning disabled child plays he can try solutions and new approaches to these difficulties which affect him. He can improve his sense of worth and well being. He is functioning in a situation over which he has some measure of control and independence. He has choices and a sense of joy and fulfillment. As the young child plays, the learning disabilities teacher, as observer, can assess the progress that he has made toward the socially defined acceptable levels of competence and curricular demands. By including play in the curriculum, the teacher taps this natural process in the best interests of the child. In order for a teacher to observe this process, the child needs a sufficient amount of time to become engrossed in a play situation and to carry through a theme. These statements are based on the writer's clinical and empirical experience over the past five years. In the following section some examples of child's play in action are given.

In recent classroom observations of 20 four- and five-year olds with two teachers, these typical children were observed to require little or no teacher direction to carry on play themes lasting 20 minutes or more. Elaborate airports and space stations were developed from available props (a garage and cars, planes, spaceship) and long mutual dialogs and cooperation occurred. This elaborate play theme sustained by five boys with no direct or indirect teacher involvement — in supplying themes, language, or mediating disputes — occurred amidst the flurry of art activity. Art activities were both sponge and brush painting, valentine preparation (each of these activities were limited to two at a time), one large drawing table seating six to eight children filled for the 20 minutes. Additionally, Legos, puzzles, and intricate shape blocks were available but not used on this day. Pillows under the piano, housekeeping corner, musical instruments, and science materials were also available for exploration. The productive level of interaction and purposeful play was maintained by the children on this observation day even with the preceding excitement of a cat who came to visit for show and tell, a planned party, and another special event.

A contrast can be drawn in another observation which was made in a self-contained classroom for severely disabled children of ages four, five, and six. In this class there are two teachers and two aides for the group of eight children (15 is the capacity for this program; enrollment has declined this year). A speech and language therapist is a part of the program for two half-days per week. In a scheduled half hour play period, the longest sustained play occurred at the climber. Two boys, with a third boy moving in and out of the theme which loosely centered around the concept of a construction site, based at the climber, engaged in associative interaction for a period of approximately 20 minutes. During this time, one teacher was constantly involved as a facilitator of the play. She suggested additional props, expanded the theme, and served as interpreter of the inarticulate language of one of the players to the others. Props move freely in this room and adaptations of housekeeping items for construction site purposes were suggested by the teacher. Costumes were adapted by the children and the teacher for the roles; and limits were set — Superman was ruled on vacation for the day when the long scarves came out. At the same time that the climber activity occurred, two boys played with a variety of blocks and cars on the floor with one aide (not sustained, but wandering away occasionally). One girl played in the house, non-verbally by herself. (The other girl was absent.) The remaining boy looked at books with the second teacher, primarily.

The contrast between the typical room and the special education room is sharp and clearly distinct on a number of bases. Included in the differences are the activity level, the stimulus variety, the language utilized, the qualitative level of thematic play and the amount and kind of teacher structuring and intervention necessary. While the typical situation might offer a goal for aspiration and hope and a yardstick for judging capabilities of the young learning disabled child's readiness for the mainstream, the heartening aspect of the contrast is that the severely disabled children also were playing and learning. The teachers, with much thought and structure devoted to program development, have created an environment where the special education preschool children were developing a sense of mastery and self-importance, as well as experiencing opportunities for choice and pleasure.

Diagnostic descriptions of two of the children, in brief, follow:

> One boy won't play in the doll corner (although he played there last year). He feels the sex role stereotype against such activity; he chooses to play alone, avoids small motor activity, including the moderately sized kindergarten blocks, and chooses sand and pull toys. He is six years old and has severe motor difficulties as well as extreme difficulties in language production.
>
> Another boy (the reader of the books) doesn't play, chooses to sit by an adult or to participate in music (when it is available). He is five and speaks less than ten words.

DIAGNOSTIC AND MONITORING PROCEDURES UTILIZED IN THE CURRICULAR STUDY OF PLAY

From research and clinical practice there are three basic techniques for the study of the young child's play which seem most applicable to the preschool learning disabilities classroom situation, both for diagnostic and monitoring purposes. These techniques include "time sampling" of classroom behavior according to categories of activity: social interaction, materials used, other behaviorally defined variables; "structured play interviews" utilizing set procedures, materials, conducted individually or in groups; and "anecdotal note recording" followed by an analysis of the streams of behavior or comparison to selected categories of behavior.

"Time sampling" procedures require the selection of variable criteria, and a plan for implementation of the observational system. Recent research studies utilizing this approach have focused primarily on the observation of social interaction styles and patterns, to examine a given child or the classroom group interactions with others. Parten's (1932) description of social interaction categories have been employed as variables. Parten described the developmental continuum of social interaction as moving from solitary to parallel to associative to cooperative. The continuum begins with the infant/toddler style of interaction, where the play of normal children can be observed as being predominately characterized as alone or side-by-side interactions. This parallel play contains independent play themes that may occasionally overlap in the sharing of materials. Associative play beginning in the preschool years is described as the beginning stage of mutual peer interaction. At the most developed level of peer interaction in the preschool years, children interact with reciprocity to maintain and elaborate on agreed upon themes and games. These definitions have been variously utilized by researchers in recent years (cf. Guralnick, 1978; Rogers-Warren, 1981; Rubin, 1978).

Application of the time sampling technique for the learning disabilities teacher includes the identification of a child or group of children to be studied. The development of a plan of observation, which would include procedures for time sampling, choice of time interval, and a plan to systematically observe the target child or children in all portions of the play period — the beginning, middle, and end — is also essential. Teachers utilizing this approach should plan to gather the time samples for a period of at least one month before attempting to formulate conclusions about the child's behavior. This approach is applicable to self-contained and mainstreamed classrooms. It requires careful study of the definitions and underlying social behavioral concepts, practice of the mechanics of observation and careful adherence to the established definitions and procedures.

"Structured play interviews" evolved from clinical practice and research traditions in play therapy which seek to examine the social/emotional or cognitive maturity of individual children or of small groups of children. Such approaches from the clinical field incorporate the use of standard materials such as dolls, doll house, telephone, blocks, play dough. These materials are usually set out in a small room and a selected child is given the opportunity to explore and interact with the materials for a period of 20 to 30 minutes. In this approach, the interviewer is given directions beforehand about the extent of verbal and non-verbal interaction that can be supplied. The interviewer records language and actions either through notes or audio or video. Sometimes mothers accompany children into the interview, if the focus of the interview is mother-child interaction. Following the interview, the protocol or record is analyzed for the degree of social/emotional and cognitive maturity based on a comparison to developmental norms and indices of emotional health (cf. Schaefer 1976).

In the study of the curricular effect of a Piagetian approach to teaching, free form materials have been supplied to small groups of children. No specific directions have been supplied for the use of these materials and observers have recorded both cognitive creativity and group structure (Duckworth 1973).

In applying these techniques to the study of child's play, the learning disabilities teacher must have a thorough grounding in the underlying concepts, carefully apply the established procedures, be prepared to abandon the approach should a crisis arise, and be cautious in generalizing results. This approach to assessment of preschool learning disabled children may supply useful baseline data on children new to the program and might be a fruitful one for examining puzzling group interactions, freeing the children from the classroom situation, and providing opportunity for observation in a standard setting. This approach would seem to be most usable by the resource specialist and the self-contained learning disabilities classroom teacher who seek to unlock the diagnostic parameters of the severely disabled child.

"Anecdotal note recordings" is probably the most used and most familiar technique for observations made by classroom teachers of all types. These techniques are used for research purposes as well. Such an approach provides a rich source of data about individual children. Generally in application a child is the focus of observation for a minimum of 10 to 15 minutes. During this time the observer records, exactly, the activity of the child at focus, the materials used, the language, and social interaction. Following a series of observations collected in this manner, conclusions are formulated about the child's maturity. Sometimes the records are subjected to an analysis by comparison to pre-determined categories (cf. Cohen and Stern 1978). For example, a series of studies have examined the dramatic play characteristics of young children and compared the play to the definitions of Smilansky (1968) for sociodramatic characteristics. These characteristics delineate the child's use of language and manipulation of symbols and are thought to be indicative of cognitive performance.

Although the anecdotal approach to observation and diagnostic assessment is familiar to teachers, it is an approach that may be frequently misused. In order to be an objective record of the child's performance, the teacher must withhold judgment while observing, or clearly separate interpretative comments from descriptive material. Frequently only conclusions are recorded. Over time, the descriptive statements may yield different interpretations than the original conclusion. The recording of conclusions alone will thus mask important diagnostic clues or lose them completely. Sometimes teachers utilize the anecdotal record primarily to build support for a viewpoint about a child. Thus, only the positive or negative behavior which the teacher wishes to document is recorded and the case built. Applied in a manner to avoid selection of specific observer bias, this approach can be applied by the teacher in settings serving the complete continuum of from least to most restrictive environments. It is a procedure that lends itself to routine use to supplement the formal test and curricular data.

SUMMARY

Play is the medium through which the young child develops a sense of mastery of his environment, a feeling of competence. Through play he can try on roles and solve situations that expand his awareness of the real world and his ability to cope with the demands (Erikson 1963). As the child plays, the teacher, as observer, can assess the progress that he has made toward the socially defined acceptable levels of competence.

The child's play reflects his stage of development; it is his natural mode of functioning (Peller 1954; Freud 1965).

By looking at the child's play, the learning disabilities teacher can form some conclusions about his stage of development and thus modify her curriculum accordingly. Examples of specific information which the learning disabilities teacher can observe as the child plays include: body movement, dramatic solutions which the child utilizes for solution of his life problems, decision making strategies, the child's perceived self-concept, perceptual skill development, playfulness and creativity, prosocial skill development, social interaction patterns.

There are three basic methods which are applicable to assessment of child's play by learning disabilities teachers. These methods are time sampling on a longitudinal or planned interval basis, the structured interview, and anecdotal note recording. While these methods are relatively straightforward and adaptible to the busy teacher's schedule, careful preparation and background study of theory and methods as well as appropriate attention to the limits of generalizability should, of course, be kept uppermost in mind as learning disabilities teachers employ this rich and natural technique for assessing and monitoring child behavior in a multidimensional fashion.

REFERENCES

Berlyne, D. D. "Laughter, humor, and play." In G. Lindzey and E. Aronson, eds. *The handbook of social psychology*, Vol. 3 (2nd ed.). Reading, Mass.: Addison Wesley, 1969, pp. 795-852.

Bruner, J. "Nature and uses of immaturity." *American Psychologist* 27 (1972): 1-28.

Bryan, J. H. "Social behaviors of learning disabled children."In J. Gottlieb and S. Strichart, eds. *Developmental theory and research in learning disabilities.* Baltimore, Md.: University Park Press, 1981.

Cohen, D. H. and V. Stern, *Observing and recording the behavior of young children.* 2nd ed. New York: Teachers College Press, 1978.

Ellis, J. J. *Why people play.* Englewood Cliffs, N.J.: Prentice Hall, 1973.

Duckworth, E. "The having of wonderful ideas." In M. Schwebel, and J. Raph, eds. *Piaget in the classroom.* New York: Basic Books, 1973.

Erikson, E. *Childhood and Society.* New York: Norton, 1963.

Farnham-Diggory, S. *Learning Disabilities: A Psychological Perspective* . Cambridge, Mass.: Harvard University Press, 1978.

Freud, A. *Normality and Pathology in Childhood: Assessments of Development*. New York: International Universities Press, 1965.

Gallagher, J. J., ed. *The Application of Child Development Research to Exceptional Children*. Reston, Va.: Council for Exceptional Children, 1975.

Goffman, E. *Stigma: Notes on the management of a spoiled identity*. Englewood Cliffs, N.J.: Prentice-Hall, 1963.

Guralnick, M. J. "Integrated preschools as educational and therapeutic environments: Concepts, design, and analysis." In *Early intervention and the integration of handicapped and nonhandicapped children*. Baltimore, Md.: University Park Press, 1978.

Hobbs, N., ed. *The futures of children*. San Francisco: Jossey-Bass, 1975.

Issacs, S. *Social development in young children*. New York: Harcourt, Brace, 1933.

Johnson, D., and H. Myklebust. *Learning Disabilities: Educational Principles and Practices*. New York: Grune & Stratton, 1967.

Lerner, J. W. *Children with Learning Disabilities: Theories, Diagnoses, and Strategies*, 3rd ed. Boston: Houghton Mifflin, 1981.

Millar, S. *The Psychology of Play*. London: Pelican, 1968.

Mogford, K. "The play of handicapped children." In B. Tizard and D. Harvey, *Biology of Play*. Philadelphia: Lippincott, 1977.

Morse, W., ed. *Humanistic teaching for exceptional children*. Syracuse: Syracuse University Press, 1979.

Neumann, E. *The Elements of Play*. New York: MSS Information, 1971.

Parten, M. D. "Social participation among preschool children." *Journal of Abnormal and Social Psychology* 27 (1932): 243-269.

Peller, L. E. "Libidinal phases, ego development, and play." *Psychoanalytical Study of the Child* 9 (1954): 178-193.

Piaget, J. *Play, Dreams and Imitation in Childhood*. New York: Norton, 1962.

Rogers-Warren, A. K., T. R. Ruggles, N. L. Peterson, and A. Y. Cooper, "Playing and Learning Together: Patterns of Social Interaction in Handicapped and Nonhandicapped Children." *Journal of the Division for Early Childhood* 3 (1981): 51-63.

Rubin, K. H., *et al.* "Free play behaviors in preschool and kindergarten children." *Child Development* (1978).

Schaeffer, C. E., ed. *Therapeutic use of child's play*. New York: Aronson, 1976.

Smilansky, S. *The effects of sociodramatic play on disadvantaged preschool children*. New York: Wiley, 1968.

Valentine, C. W. "A study of the beginnings and significance of play in infancy." *British Journal of Educational Psychology* 8 (1938): 285-306.

White, R. W. "Motivation reconsidered: The concept of competence." *Psychology Review* 66 (1959): 297-333.

SUGGESTED BIBLIOGRAPHY ON CHILDREN'S PLAY

Caney, S. *Playbook*. New York: Workman, 1975.

Caplan, F., and T. Caplan, *The Power of Play*. New York: Anchor, 1974.

Fein, G. "Play and acquisition of symbols." In L. Katz ed. *Current topics in early childhood education, V. 2*. Norwood, N.J.: Ablex, 1979.

Frost, J., and B. Klein, *Children's play and playgrounds*. Boston: Allyn and Bacon, 1979.

Garvey, C. *Play*. Cambridge: Harvard University Press, 1977.

Gould, R. *Child Studies through Fantasy*. New York: Quadrangle, 1972.

Hartley, R., L. Frank, and R. Goldenson. *Understanding Children's Play*. New York: Columbia University Press, 1952.

Matterson, E. *Games for the Very Young*. New York: American Heritage, 1969.

———. *Play and Playthings for the Preschool Child*. New York: Penguin, 1967.

Piers, M., and G. Landau. *The Gift of Play*. New York: Walker, 1980.

———. *Play: The Child Strives for Self-realization*. Washington, D.C.: National Association for the Education of Young Children, 1971.

Rubin, K. *Children's Play*. New Directions for Child Development, 9 (1980).

Sharp, E. *Thinking is Child's Play*. New York: Dutton, 1969.

Singer, J. L. *The Child's World of Make Believe*. New York: Academic Press, 1973.

Sponseller, D. *Play as a Learning Medium*. Washington, D.C.: National Association for Education of Young Children, 1974.

Wolfgang, C. *Helping aggressive and passive preschoolers through play*. Columbus, O.: Charles E. Merrill, 1977.

15

Metamemory Development
in Learning Disabled Children

Mary L. Trepanier and Christine M. Casale

DIFFERENCES IN memory performance have been reported between young and old normal children and between learning disabled and same-aged normal children. A similarity between the memory performance of younger, normal children (4-6 years) and learning disabled children (7-14 years) has been suggested (Ornstein, Naus, and Liberty 1975; Torgesen 1977). Poor memory performance in both groups has been attributed to a failure to use efficient strategies, such as rehearsal and categorization, rather than to a reduced memory capacity. Additionally, both groups consistently have exhibited a general insensitivity to memory tasks, or, a failure to "differentiate" occasions that require the active use of strategies (Appel, Cooper, McCarrell, Sims-Knight, Yussin, and Flavell 1972; Hallahan and Reeve 1980; Torgesen 1977).

Recently, the development of normal children's understanding of their memory processes, or metamemory, has been investigated. Findings have shown similarities and differences between younger and older normal children. Thus, the following questions arise: (1) do learning disabled and normal children exhibit similarities and differences in metamemory development? and (2) does learning disabled children's metamemory development, like memory performance, parallel that found in normal children? The primary purpose of this research was to compare the metamemory ability of learning disabled and same-aged normal children. The metamemory areas selected for study were memory ability, immediate vs. delayed recall, memory estimation, length of study time, number of items, objects vs. designs, and use of rehearsal and categorization strategies.

The metamemory ability of learning disabled children has been investigated by Torgesen (1979). Although some similarities and differences in metamemory between good and poor readers were found, a major limitation of this study was its use of a single age group (CA 9 years). This fact prevented an examination of age differences in learning disabled children's metamemory. Thus, the question of developmental differences is, as yet, an open one.

Similarities between young and old normal children's metamemory have been found. Young children (CA 5-6 years) have reported that although they sometimes forgot things, generally they remembered well (Kreutzer, Leonard, and Flavel 1975). Recognizing the importance of immediate recall, they would prefer to call immediately after hearing a phone number rather than to get a drink first. Understanding that length of study time could influence recall, they would choose five minutes to study rather than one minute (Kreutzer *et al.* 1975). Young children also realized that the number of items and their familiarity with the items (those easily named) could influence their memory performance.

Developmental differences in normal children's metamemory have been found. Compared to older children, younger children unrealistically overestimated their memory ability (Flavell, Friedrichs, and Hoyt 1979; Markman 1973; Yussen and Levy 1975). Additionally, they suggested the use of rehearsal and categorization as mnemonic strategies less often than older children (Kreutzer *et al.* 1975; Moynahan 1973).

Given these similarities and differences in normal children, it was anticipated that learning disabled children's understanding would be similar in memory ability, immediate vs. delayed recall, study time, number of items, and objects vs. designs. Differences were anticipated in memory estimation, rehearsal, and categorization.

METHOD

Subjects

A total of 100 subjects, 50 learning disabled and 50 normal children, were selected from five schools within a large metropolitan area. Subjects were matched for age (6-4 years to 15-8 years, $\overline{X}$ = 10-3 years, SD = 2-3 years) and sex (16 females and 34 males in each group). The learning disabled children were selected from five resource rooms. These subjects had been identified by an Educational Planning and Placement Committee using Michigan's state guidelines. Learning disabled subjects' mean score on the Peabody Picture Vocabulary Test (PPVT) was 105.16 (SD = 12.09). On the Visual Sequential Memory subtest of the Illinois Test of Psycholinguistic Abilities (ITPA), standard scores ranged from 25 to 64 with a mean of 35.34 (SD = 8.13). Simple scores on the Memory for Objects subtest of the Detroit Test of Learning Abilities (Detroit) ranged from 27 to 64 with a mean of 44 (SD = 7.99).

Normal subjects drawn from the same schools were also administered the PPVT ($\overline{X}$ = 107.42, SD = 12.33), the ITPA (standard score range: 31−54, $\overline{X}$ = 38.56, SD = 5.64) and the Detroit (simple score range: 36−63, $\overline{X}$ = 48, SD = 6.02). The groups differed significantly in memory performance [ITPA ($F(1)$ = 5.284, p < .05); Detroit ($F(1)$ = 7.910, p < .01)].

Both the learning disabled and the normal groups were further subdivided into two age groups. The study included four groups of 25: the learning disabled old (age range $10-0$ years to $15-8$ years, $\overline{X} = 12.0$ years), the learning disabled young (age range: $6-4$ years to $9-9$ years, $\overline{X} = 8-3$ years), the normal old (age range: $9-9$ years to $15-8$ years, $\overline{X} = 12-1$ years), and the normal young (age range: $6-4$ years to $9-8$ years, $\overline{X} = 8-3$ years).

Procedures

Both learning and disabled and normal subjects were tested individually by trained research assistants in two sessions. At the first session, the measures of intelligence and memory were administered. During the second session, subjects responded to a metamemory interview which included questions from the research by Kreutzer *et al*. (1975), Flavell *et al*. (1970), Moynahan (1973), and original questions. The order of item presentation was random. A description of the metamemory interview follows:

I. *Memory Ability/Memory Estimation*
Examiner asked: Sometimes I forget things. (1) Do you forget? (2) Do you remember things well — are you a good rememberer? (3) Can you remember better than your friends, or do they remember more than you? For example, if I gave you 10 things to look at quickly and remember and you remembered six of them, how many do you think your friends would remember? (4) Sometimes although a person is a good rememberer, he can still remember some things better than others. Do you remember some kinds of things better than others? (5) Are there some kinds of things that are really hard to remember?

II. *Immediate versus Delayed Recall: Auditory Memory*
Examiner asked: (1) If you wanted to phone your friend and someone told you the phone number, would it make any difference if you called right away after you heard the number or if you got a drink of water first? (2) Why? (3) What do you do when you want to remember a phone number?

III. *Immediate versus Delayed Recall: Visual Memory*
Examiner placed a series of 15 black and white pictures of common objects in random order in front of the subject and then asked: (1) If I showed you a series of pictures such as these would it make a difference if you were asked to recall the pictures right away or if you took a walk first? (2) What do you do when you want to remember the group of pictures?

IV. *Study Time*

Examiner showed the subject 20 black and white pictures of common objects placed randomly. Examiner asked: The other day I asked two children to look at and learn some pictures because I wanted to see how well they could remember. I asked them how much time they would like to have to learn the pictures before I would take them away and ask them how many they could remember. One child said 1 minute. The other child said a longer time, 5 minutes. (1) Why do you think he wanted as long as 5 minutes? (2) Which child remembered the most, the one who studied 1 minute, or the one who studied 5 minutes? (3) Why? (4) And what would you do, study 5 minutes or 1 minute? (5) Why?

V. *Number of Items*

Examiner showed the subjects four sets of cards in a random order. The 21 cm. x 29 cm. cards had 3, 6, 9, or 18 line drawings of common unrelated objects. The following questions were then asked: (1) If you were asked to remember the items that are on the cards, which card would be the hardest or most difficult to remember? (2) Why? (3) Which would be the next easiest? (4) Why? (5) Which would be the next easiest? (6) Why? (7) Which would be the next easiest? (8) Why?

VI. *Memory Estimation*

Examiner showed the subject a series of ten strips displaying pictures of common objects. The number of items on the strips increased from one to ten items. The examiner asked while showing each strip: (1) Do you think you could remember this strip if I asked you to try to remember it and then I covered it up? After the first *no* response the examiner discontinued the presentation of strips and asked: (2) Why would that strip be difficult to remember?

VII. *Objects versus Designs and Use of Rehearsal Strategy*

The examiner showed the subject two sets of line drawings with each drawing approximately 5 cm. × 7 cm. in size. One set was composed of common objects (all of which were easily labeled), while the other set was composed of free-form designs (not easily labeled). This task was conducted with sets of 2 items and with sets of 5 items. Subjects were asked for each: One day I asked a boy/girl to remember this set of pictures (gesturing to the common objects) and then on another day to remember these pictures (the designs). (1) Which group of pictures would be easier to remember or would they both be the same? (2) Why? (3) How would you remember the pictures? Would you do anything special to remember? For the 5 items comparison only: (4) Would saying the names of the pictures help you to remember either set of pictures? (5) Why?

VIII. *Categorization*

The examiner showed the subject two sets of pictures of common objects. The 5 cm. × 6 cm. black and white, line drawings were displayed on 21 cm. x 29 cm. cards. The task was repeated for: (1) two sets of 6 items (one set with one category — (kitchen items) — and one set not categorized), and (2) two sets of 9 items (one set with two categories — (clothes, people) — and one set not categorized). Subjects were asked the following questions for each condition: (1) If you were asked to look and try to remember the items on each card which would be easier to remember? (2) Why? (3) How would you remember the objects? Would you do anything special?

RESULTS

Responses were scored in a manner comparable to other metamemory research (Kreutzer *et al.* 1975). Reliability of scoring was assessed by having two judges independently score 15 protocols. The interjudge reliability across the metamemory measures was .96.

Omnibus chi-square analyses were used to compare the metamemory responses of the four groups. Insignificant omnibus chi squares suggested no relationship between age, type (learning disabled or normal) and metamemory response. However, significant chi square plus additional analyses suggested developmental differences between the groups. Those metamemory areas where no relationship was found are reported first.

Memory Ability

A clear majority of subjects in the four groups responded that they sometimes forgot things (84-100 percent), they were good rememberers (80-92 percent), and they found some things easy and other things difficult to remember (100 percent). The types of things that all groups suggested as difficult to remember were similar. The chi square analysis for each of these questions was insignificant.

Immediate versus Delayed Recall

A majority of subjects (56-76 percent) in all groups recognized a difference between calling immediately after hearing a number and getting a drink of water first. They also appropriately justified their responses (56-88 percent).

Similarly, subjects realized the effect of taking a walk before recalling a set of 20 pictures (80-88 percent). The omnibus chi square for each of the questions was insignificant.

Study Time

The majority of subjects in all groups recognized that studying for five minutes was preferrable to studying for one minute (72-92 percent). Omnibus chi-square analyses suggested no relationship between the groups and their choices or their justifications for choices.

Number of Items

A majority of subjects in all groups correctly sequenced a series of 3, 6, 9, and 18 item pictures according to difficulty (84-94 percent). They also appropriately justified, their response, i.e., referred to number (76-94 percent). Insignificant omnibus chi squares suggested no relationship between age, learning type, and the ability to recognize the influence of number of items on task difficulty.

Objects versus Designs: Choice and Labeling

Collapsing across the two and five item tasks, subjects (88-100 percent) correctly identified objects as easier to remember than designs. Subjects (80-96 percent) also stated that saying the names of the pictures would help recall. Omnibus chi squares for these questions were not significant.

Categorization: Choice

Given two sets of pictures, subjects chose the set of related pictures as easier to recall than the set of unrelated pictures (60-70 percent). An omnibus chi square was not significant.

Besides these similarities, differences among the four groups were found on the metamemory interview. A description of these differences follow.

Memory Ability/Memory Estimation

Subjects estimated the number of items their friends might remember if they could remember six items. A one-way analysis of variance approached significance (F (3) = 2.58, p = .058). However, the group means did not adequately reflect the quality of the subjects' responses. When responses were categorized as accurate (an estimate of 3, 4, 5, 6, 7, or 8) or inaccurate (an estimate of 0, 1, 2, 9, or 10), a significant omnibus chi square was obtained (omnibus χ^2 (4) = 12.354, p < .05). To determine the source of the significance, cell chi squares were converted into a standardized residual with an associated probability level. The standardized residual can be interpreted similarly to a z score with zero as the mean and a standard deviation of one (Everitt 1977). Standardized residuals suggested that the younger learning disabled group were significantly less accurate (residual = −5.32, p < .001) and that the older normal group was significantly more accurate (residual = 4.34, p < .001). The old learning disabled and the young normal groups were equivalent.

Memory Estimation

Subjects were asked whether they thought they could remember a series of ten strips which increased in length from one to ten items. Subjects estimated the longest strip they could successfully recall. Analysis of variance of the four groups was not significant.

Descriptive analysis of the memory estimation responses showed little variability for the normal old group, the normal young group, and the learning disabled old group. By comparison, the distribution for the learning disabled young group was more disperse. Responses were then categorized into accurate estimates (estimates of 3, 4, 5, 6, 7, 8 items) or inaccurate estimates (estimates of 0, 1, 2, 9, 10 items). The result of an omnibus chi square was significant (χ^2 (4) = 15.015, p < .001). While only 4 percent of the learning disabled old, normal old, and normal young groups gave an inaccurate estimate, 32 percent of the learning disabled young group gave an inaccurate estimate. In fact, 20 percent of the learning disabled young group responded that they could remember all *ten* items.

Subjects who stated an inability to remember all ten strips were subsequently asked the reason. An omnibus chi square was significant (χ^2 (4) = 17.943, p < .001). An equivalent percentage of subjects in the learning disabled old (92 percent), normal old (96 percent), and normal young groups (92 percent) correctly justified their response. However, only 55 percent of the learning disabled young group gave an appropriate reason. Thus, the learning disabled young group gave significantly more inaccurate estimates of their memory recall (residual = −6.72, p < .001) and more inaccurate justifications (residual = −8.52, p < .001).

Objects versus Designs: Rehearsal Strategy

All groups chose objects as easier to remember than designs. However, the appropriateness of their rationale for choice differed. An appropriate rationale referred to the more inherent labeling quality of the objects. An omnibus chi square across the two and five item tasks was significant ($\chi^2 (4) = 15.525$, $p < .001$).

By comparison the normal old children gave significantly more appropriate reasons (residual $= 4.77, p < .001$), while the learning disabled old and normal young groups were equivalent. The learning disabled young children gave significantly less appropriate reasons (residual $= -6.06 p < .001$).

Subjects were then asked how they would remember the objects. Responses were scored as a strategic response (e.g., referred to rehearsal, grouping, writing, drawing, or associating) or a nonstrategic response (e.g., looking, don't know). A significant omnibus chi square was obtained ($\chi^2 (4) = 15.525$, $p < .001$). The normal old group gave significantly more strategic responses (residual $= 5.1, p < .001$) compared to all other groups. In addition the normal old group (52 percent) suggested rehearsal, the most appropriate strategy, more often than the learning disabled old (32 percent), the normal young (32 percent), or the learning disabled young (30 percent) groups.

When further prompted about rehearsal, the majority of all subjects agreed that saying the names would help recall. However, not all subjects appropriately justified why it would help. When responses were scored as either appropriate or inappropriate, differences between the groups were apparent: normal old, 38 percent; normal young, 34 percent; learning disabled old, 28 percent; learning disabled young, 16 percent. An omnibus chi square was significant ($\chi^2 (4) = 11.33, p < .05$).

CATEGORIZATION

Subjects in all four groups chose the categorized objects as easier than the unrelated objects (60-70 percent). However, when asked to justify their choice, differences between the groups were seen. More appropriate justifications were found in the normal old group (57 percent) than in the other groups (learning disabled old, 38 percent; learning disabled young, 36 percent; normal young, 36 percent). When asked to suggest a strategy for remembering categorized items, the learning disabled young group gave fewer strategies (46 percent) than the other groups (normal old, 70 percent; learning disabled old, 70 percent; normal young, 68 percent). Specifically, the younger learning disabled children suggested categorization, the most appropriate strategy, less often (8 percent) than the other three groups (normal old, 34 percent; learning disabled old, 30 percent; normal young, 18 percent).

DISCUSSION

The results of this study suggested that learning disabled and normal children were similar in several metamemory areas. Learning disabled children, like normal children, understood they sometimes forgot things but that generally they remembered well. They also understood the facilitative effects of: (1) immediate recall, (2) familiar items (objects vs. designs), (3) longer study time, and (4) fewer items upon memory performance. Given the findings of research with very young normal children, these results were anticipated.

Developmental differences in the normal population were reported in the metamemory areas of memory estimation, rehearsal, and categorization. Differences between learning disabled and normal children were anticipated in these areas. The results support these predictions.

Learning disabled and normal children differed in their understanding of the boundaries or limitations of short-term memory. Specifically, young learning disabled children (6-9 years), like even younger normal children (4-6 years), gave more inaccurate estimates of memory ability. In fact, several stated they could remember all *10* items even if given a short study time.

Learning disabled and normal children also differed in their understanding of the facilitative effects of using a rehearsal strategy. Learning disabled children gave fewer appropriate responses to the questions: (1) why objects were easier to recall than designs, and (2) why saying the name of objects might help recall. Learning disabled children also offered rehearsal as an appropriate strategy for object recall less often than normal children.

Finally, differences between learning disabled and normal children's understanding of categorization were found. Similar to the findings on the rehearsal questions, learning disabled children gave fewer appropriate justifications for the recall ease of categorized items compared to unrelated items. They suggested categorization as an appropriate mnemonic strategy less often than normal children.

Metamemory areas of difference are profiled in Figure 15.1.

The following statements summarize the pattern of responses of the four groups:

1. The response profiles were parallel across all items. All groups found the same item easy, and similarly, all groups found the same items difficult.

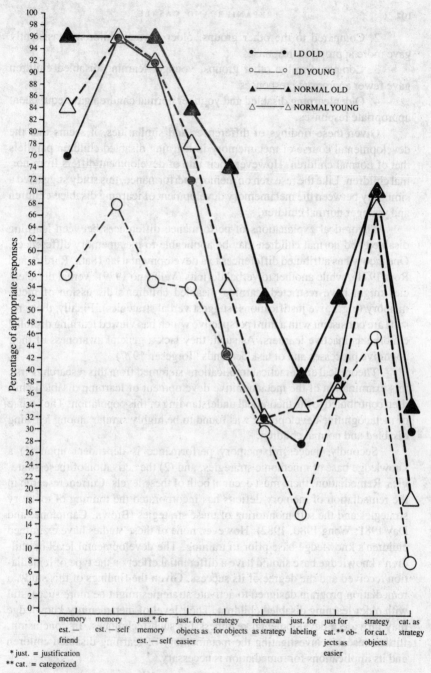

Figure 15.1. Percentage of appropriate responses to metamemory items by group.

2. Compared to the other groups, older normal children consistently gave more appropriate responses.

3. Compared to the other groups, younger learning disabled children gave fewer appropriate responses.

4. Older learning disabled and younger normal children gave equivalent appropriate responses.

Given these findings of differences and similarities, it seems that the developmental course of metamemory in learning disabled children parallels that of normal children. However, their rate of development differs from normal children. Like the research on memory performance, this study suggested a similarity between the metamemory development of learning disabled children and younger normal children.

Theoretical explanations of performance differences between learning disabled and normal children may be applicable to metamemory differences. One theory has attributed differences to a developmental lag (Satz, Rardin, and Ross 1971), while another to verbal deficits (Vellutino 1979). Verbal deficiencies might have restricted learning disabled children's discussion of metamemory (e.g., give justifications, suggest verbal strategies). Finally, these results are consistent with a third perspective which has viewed learning disabled children as inactive learners. As such, they lack a general awareness of their cognitive processes and of task demands (Torgesen 1977).

Theoretical and practical implications stemmed from this research. First, this examination of the metacognitive development of learning disabled children contributed to the theoretical understanding of this population. The course of metacognitive development was found to be highly similar among learning disabled and normal children.

Secondly, successful memory performance is dependent upon (1) a knowledge base of mnemonic strategies, and (2) the activation of these strategies. Remediation, then, must occur at both of these levels. Current research in the remediation of memory deficits has incorporated the training of memory strategies and the self-monitoring of these strategies (Brown, Campione, and Day 1981; Wong 1980, 1982). However, none of these studies have examined children's knowledge base prior to training. The developmental level of children's knowledge base should have a differential effect on the type of remediation received and the degree of its success. Given the findings of this study, a remediation program designed to activate strategies might be more successful with older learning disabled children. Their level of metamemory knowledge may provide a developmental readiness for such techniques. In conclusion, further research investigating the metamemory of learning disabled children and its implications for remediation is necessary.

REFERENCES

Appel, L. F., R. G. Cooper, N. McCarrell, J. Sims-Knight, S. R. Yussen, and J. H. Flavell. The development of the distinction between perceiving and memorizing. *Child Development*, 1972, *43*, 1365-1381.

Brown, A. L., J. C. Campione, and J. D. Day. Learning to learn: On training students to learn from tests. *Educational Researcher*, 1981, *10*, 14-21.

Everitt, B. S. *The analysis of contingency tables.* New York: John Wiley, 1977.

Flavell, J. H., A. G. Friedrichs, J. D. Hoyt. Developmental changes in memorization processes. *Cognitive Psychology*, 1970, *1*, 324-340.

Hallahan, D. P. and R. E. Reeve. Selective attention and distractibility. In B. K. Keogh, ed. *Advances in special education: Vol 1.* Greenwich, Conn.: JAI Press, 1980.

Kreutzer, M. A., C. Leonard, and J. H. Flavell. An interview study of children's knowledge about memory. *Monographs of the Society for Research in Child Development*, 1975, *40*, (1, Serial no. 159).

Markman, E. "Factors affecting the young child's ability to monitor his memory." Doctoral dissertation, University of Pennsylvania, 1973.

Moynahan, Eileen D. The development of knowledge concerning the effect of categorization upon free recall. *Child Development*, 1973, *44*, 238-246.

Ornstein, P. A., M. J. Naus, and B. P. Stone. Rehearsal training and developmental differences in memory. *Developmental Psychology*, 1977, *13*, 15-24.

Satz, P., D. Rardin, and J. Ross. An evaluation of a theory of specific developmental dyslexia. *Child Development*, 1971, *42*, 2009-2021.

Torgesen, J. R. The role of nonspecific factors in the task performance of learning disabled children: A theoretical assessment. *Journal of Learning Disabilities*, 1977, *10*, 33-39.

———. Factors related to poor performance on memory tasks in reading disabled children. *Learning Disability Quarterly*, 1979, *2*, 17-23.

Vellutino, F. *Dyslexia: Theory and research.* Cambridge, Mass.: The MIT Press, 1979.

Wong, B. Activating the inactive learner: Use of questions/prompts to enhance comprehension and retention of implied information in learning disabled children. *Learning Disability Quarterly*, 1980, *13*, 29-37.

———. Strategic behaviors in selecting retrieval cues in gifted, normal achieving and learning disabled children. *Journal of Learning Disabilities*, 1982, *15*, 33-37.

Yussen, Stephen R., and Victor M. Levy, Jr. Developmental changes in knowledge about different retrieval problems. *Developmental Psychology*, 1977, *13*, 114-120.

ACADEMICS AND BEYOND

was composed in 10-point Compugraphic Times Roman and leaded two points,
with Times Roman display type by Emerald Graphics;
printed sheet-fed offset on 50-pound, acid-free Glatfelter offset,
adhesive-bound, with 10-point Carolina covers by Wickersham Printing Co., Inc.,
and published by

SYRACUSE UNIVERSITY PRESS
SYRACUSE, NEW YORK